C000263699

STOP DREAMI...
AND START DOING

For a complete list of Management Books 2000 titles,
visit our web-site on http://www.mb2000.com

This book has been produced for people considering establishing their 'own-businesses'. It has been carefully prepared but is not necessarily exhaustive and is intended as a general guide only. It is no substitute for specialist professional assistance and those seriously considering starting their 'own-business' are strongly advised to seek their own legal, accounting, and other relevant advice before committing themselves.

Whilst every effort has been made to ensure the accuracy of the information contained in this book, changes may have been made in the law or elsewhere following publication. The publisher and the author make no representations or warranties about the accuracy or completeness of the contents of this book and specifically disclaim any implied warranties. Neither the author nor the publisher can be held responsible for any losses incurred as a result of any omission or error whether for special, incidental, consequential, or other damages.

STOP DREAMING AND START DOING

Frank Thaxton

A step-by-step guide to starting your own business

2000

Copyright © Frank Thaxton 2005

All rights reserved. No part of this publication may be reproduced, stored in a retrieval system, or transmitted in any form or by any means, electronic, mechanical, photocopying, recording, or otherwise without the prior permission of the publishers.

First published in 2005 by Management Books 2000 Ltd
Forge House, Limes Road
Kemble, Cirencester
Gloucestershire, GL7 6AD, UK
Tel: +44 (0) 1285 771441
Fax: +44 (0) 1285 771055
E-mail: info@mb2000.com
Web: www.mb2000.com

Printed and bound in Great Britain by Digital Books Logistics Ltd of Peterborough

This book is sold subject to the condition that it shall not, by way of trade or otherwise, be lent, resold, hired out, or otherwise circulated without the publisher's prior consent in any form of binding or cover other than that in which it is published and without a similar condition including this condition being imposed upon the subsequent purchaser.

British Library Cataloguing in Publication Data is available

ISBN 1-85252-486-3

About the author

After completing an engineering degree at Imperial College London, Frank Thaxton started his career in manufacturing industry, where he later qualified as an accountant. After holding several senior finance roles with UK and international responsibilities, Frank moved into venture capital for 10 years, investing in smaller, entrepreneurial and start-up companies in the engineering, electronics, software, and communications industries. He formed his own consultancy business in 1985, working with many clients (individuals and companies) across a wide variety of sectors. He has advised on starting and growing businesses, mergers and acquisitions, marketing and operations, financing, business sales, as well as on employment issues. He has contributed articles on finance for the smaller firm, on starting up in business, and has given talks and run seminars in the same area.

He has more recently been involved in coaching people through the start of a new career, specialising in the area of setting up, or buying into, independent business. These have ranged from small shops and business service companies to large management buy-ins (up to £500m). He is passionate about helping people to start and run successful businesses. This book was produced to assist in this area.

Contents

Contents

Acknowledgements

Many people have helped me over the years and therefore some of their expertise is included in this book. Clients, colleagues, and friends have all contributed in their own ways and it seems invidious to mention only a few by name. Nevertheless, I would really like to thank Ian McIntyre of Maxwell Batley, who has many years' experience advising young and growing businesses on all aspects of their affairs, for comments on the legal issues. I also want to thank Elliot Harris of Chantrey Vellacott DFK, who has been closely involved in the owner-managed business sector for many years, particularly in assisting business start-ups, for providing advice in the financial and accounting area. David MacLean gave me some very useful advice in the tax area and I was enthusiastically supported whilst writing this edition by my partner Judy Proudfoot, who deserves special thanks. Leah Thaxton again provided valuable editorial advice in the later stages, for which I am very grateful, and I continue to enjoy and value the involvement of Colin Selby and Graham Mills – who were there in the beginning! There are many more names that I have not mentioned, who will know who they are, and my thanks for their contributions are no less sincere because their names are not here.

If you have any comments or suggestions for improvements in the next edition, please send them to me at the publishers info@mb2000.com, or at frankthaxton@tvpl.co.uk

1

Introduction

Having spent many years advising and coaching people who wanted to start their own businesses (the majority of whom actually went ahead and did so), I see my role as helping people realise worthwhile dreams and turn them into reality. Some dreams should stay just that, dreams – to get us through the days, especially the tough days 'on the job' but the dreams I'm talking about are those that need to be converted into success.

Covering the complete agenda for starting a new business is a major piece of work – meriting a huge volume or series of volumes. This is a small book – deliberately so. It's one to carry around and read on the train or bus, or in public places. You can write in this book, make notes on it, or even (as some have done) take out the pages and interleave them in a file with your own pages of notes. This is the start of what I hope will be the best years of your life. In a survey a few years ago of many hundreds who had read the earlier version of this book, the vast majority were very happy to have started out on their own (the survey was carried out one year plus after their business start date) and included a few who had gone back to employed work!

My aim is not to answer all of your questions or to teach you all you need to know to start out on your 'own-business'. My aim is to set out most of the key issues, to widen your perspective, to give you a more reasoned and balanced look at your own ideas, to make you wiser, and to enable you to ask more pertinent questions of more people. I hope the advice you receive is realistic, the information relevant, and that it gives you more confidence to face the exciting challenge ahead.

Notes:

At times, I have used the **masculine pronoun** ('he', 'him', or 'his') not because most 'own-businesses' are run by males, but because any other approach becomes either cumbersome or sounds affected. I have not sought to address issues that are different for men and women.

I use the word **'family'** to describe the group of people closest to you, possibly including partner, children, parents, friends. These are the people who will be interested in your progress, who can be affected by your decisions, who can improve (or make more difficult) your daily life etc.

I have also used the term **'own-business'** as a generic to cover whatever business someone may be starting – whether retail, wholesale, manufacturing, franchising or whatever. Again, this is for simplicity and straight-forwardness.

2

Personal Considerations

2.1 Introduction

So, you want to start your own business. There are many backgrounds to such a decision – an inspired view, a long-planned and saved-for event, redundancy/termination of employment, and even 'I have no other option'. In every case, it represents a new start, some new challenges, the potential for success, being your own boss, running the show, a fantastic new option, a great opportunity, a chance to learn new skills, gain huge rewards and receive 100% of them. Sounds great – or does it?

To be sure, there is a lot involved and it will not always operate in your favour. This book lists some of the main issues to be addressed, starting with the most important – you. To make a success of this new venture, a great number of issues and tasks need to be considered and decided – and you will be the one to do it. You are the one who makes the difference, you are going to make it happen, and if you don't believe in the new venture, no-one else will.

2.2 Are you the right sort of person for self-employment?

'Ninety-nine percent of the people in the world should be working for somebody.'

Why do some people go into their 'own-business', while others never go beyond talking about it? Why do some of those who 'have a go' succeed, while others fail? Although cash, effort, market crises, and luck can all play a part, personal suitability is a key factor and in many cases the only person who can judge whether or not you are suited to run your 'own-business' is you.

Here is one entrepreneur's list of *characteristics* demonstrated by people who should *not* go it alone in business:

- lazy – you should be prepared to work 80 hours a week
- compliant – if you are easily pushed around, you'll get hurt
- accepting failure – you will lose
- pessimistic
- poor judges of character.

Someone with the *potential for business success* may show the following qualities:

- prefers action to contemplation
- likes to keep close to the customer
- autonomous, flexible
- believes in getting results through people
- hands-on, value-driven operator
- concentrates effort – doesn't over-diversify
- prefers simple organisations, lean staff
- both 'loose' (doesn't breathe down staff necks, delegates real responsibility) and 'tight' (demands and gets high standards, performance, results).

Warren Avis, who built the car-hire firm, said:

'The entrepreneur loves business first, has a one-track mind, great stamina, good judgement about people and high energy levels balanced by periods of relaxation.'

So, how do you fit? If your heart sinks when comparing yourself to these profiles, don't despair. Plenty of people who don't fit them completely manage to make a reasonable living running their 'own-businesses'. Take a careful, honest look at your own temperament, abilities and circumstances and try to improve your chances of success by taking appropriate action now. Your new venture requires and deserves your commitment and perseverance to overcome the inevitable hurdles. It's refreshing to remember that success is often not about having or coming up with brilliant ideas or plans, nor about luck, but mainly about good solid hard work and determination.

2.3   What do you hope to derive from it?

Clarify the objectives for yourself and your business as truthfully as you can by writing them down and then testing them on people who know you well and whom you trust to give you candid feedback. Since you are complex, your objectives are unlikely to be simple. **Don't fool yourself.** Check whether you have clearly defined – or perhaps missed out some of – what you are looking for in each of the areas listed below and then rank your objectives in order of importance:-

Money/significant financial gain	Working hours
Risk/excitement	Stress levels
Type of work	Independence
Achievement	Power
Status	Personal relationships
Enjoyment	Other

You need also to face up to a number of possibilities.

- Your income may be reduced by more than you care to accept.
- Your working hours may well be longer.
- Life may feel more risky.
- The stress levels may increase.
- You may need to turn your hand to all of the jobs in your business, including those that you don't want.
- Your independence may be less than you wanted.
- You may need to cope with your own reactions to failure(s).
- Being the boss may give you less sense of power and freedom than you had expected.
- You may need more personal relationship skills than you thought likely.

17

To replace a full-time employed job, you will need to achieve an adequate income in each and every year and be able to provide for a satisfactory pension. If you are successful, then your net asset position should go up annually and your only financial problem will be how to minimise the tax payable when you die. Often, through poor planning, lack of analysis and misdirected effort, other financial problems arrive much earlier.

But maybe you do not want to replace a full-time job or seek a main income-generating role; you may not want or need to create significant wealth. It's just as worth-while an objective for you to seek a part-time role, to want to provide a support or second income, or to provide additional income to enhance an early pension, or to provide sufficient income to justify your own time commitment to the new venture. What does success mean to you? When will you know that the 'own-business' is working well for you? Try to define it now, in writing, with timescales.

2.4 Self-appraisal

This book does not attempt to list all of the questions that you should ask of yourself, your family, your finances and your skills to help assess your suitability for an 'own-business'. Nobody can force you to evaluate your own suitability honestly and systematically, but remember that the alternative is to find out the hard way. There are questionnaires and many books available on this subject and even the most basic of these can contain useful input to your decisions. Try the 'Entrepreneur' questionnaire at **www.careersdirect.com** which identifies some of your strengths and weaknesses for self-employment – and offers some helpful suggestions to address these.

Remember too that there is no such thing as a perfect profile for self-employment. There is also no one you can go to who can say definitively 'Yes' or 'No' to your question, 'Am I right to start my own business?' There are many characteristics required and **at this stage** perhaps the most important is to be sufficiently self-aware and to assess and cover the risks you foresee.

Discuss your strengths and weaknesses, your intentions regarding the business, and any concerns you may have with friends or colleagues. Choose people whose judgement you trust – and discuss matters comprehensively. You should also discuss your decisions and the background with those members of your family/friends who will be affected by them. You will need them 'on-side' in the coming months.

In reviewing your skills mix, don't forget that important omissions can be offset by working with, or employing, other people. It is very rare for someone individually to possess exactly, and all, the right attributes and many professional investors would not even consider a sole manager for a target investment, having a 'house rule' to invest only in management teams of two or more.

To assess yourself, try writing down some of the main tasks you carried out well in your last job, setting out why you were 'the hero' in achieving them, and what it meant to you to be performing well. Review your job satisfaction in that role and in prior roles – what went well, badly and so on. Write down your skills in some form of matrix to provide a comprehensive coverage (not just the skills you see as currently relevant, but include as many as you can – they could be relevant later); then group them. Think about skills development – how you can gain greater accomplishment in key areas – and also about enjoyment (you may be good at something which you no longer enjoy doing). List out the priorities for you in a job/role and try some form of grading for importance to you (e.g. importance gradings of 1 to 5) and then assess the scores on these items for your last employed job and for the 'own-business'. See the example shown below.

Example – personal assessment

1. Key tasks that I did
Write out the key issues that you tackled, how you did it, what made you different and gave you success – say, for 10 'projects' which were important to you. Then analyse them and see what you can learn, including your key strengths.

2. Job satisfaction
Key satisfactions for you:
Key dissatisfactions:

3. Skills

List out as many skills/attributes/experiences as you can under the following headings:

Skills   **Skills groups**   **Example/stories of using skill**

4. Priorities

Rate from your viewpoint – from 1 unimportant to 5 vital

	Job	Self-employment
Steady salary of £xx,xxx	5	Nil
Opportunity to earn more	2	4
Responsibility	5 (limited)	3 (unlimited)
Autonomy	2	5
Using my main skills	4	5
Status of role	4	3
Large department	4	1
Life goals – work/life balance	3	4
Etc …		

Add any other items that are important to you and rate them from 1 to 5.

The object of the whole exercise is to get to know yourself better – warts and all. Time spent recalling and assessing your strengths and so on can be extremely useful in highlighting services to offer clients, and areas to avoid or support. This is not a job to be rushed – so spend time on the exercise and discuss the outcomes with others who know you well.

Accept too that you can never be perfect! Seek advice from wherever you can and **listen to it**. It isn't always advisable to accept and implement all and any advice, but it is always good to listen to it. Don't take advice given as criticisms – generally people want to help and offer advice in this light – it may be too that you have not given them sufficient information to provide the advice you seek.

Another useful tip – think of engaging a mentor or coach for the first few years in your new business. It will cost you to do so, but at least you will be challenged on key issues by someone who will not (necessarily) take yes for an answer!

'Advice is least welcome where it's most needed.'

2.5 Key points

- You are the one who is going to make it happen.

- Check out your qualities for success – candidly.

- Understand, and write down, your objectives and timescales for success in this business.

- What does success mean to you?

- Involve those around you, especially your family.

- Seek other people's views (friends, associates, colleagues) – honest views on your strengths and weaknesses.

- Don't ignore honest criticism. Use it to improve your chances.

- Would you, ideally, recruit you to run this business?

- What do you want to get out of this venture? Money, prestige, power, independence? If you don't know, how will you know when you've got it?

Now add your own key points below:

- .

- .

- .

3

The Business Idea

3.1 Introduction

Your business will almost certainly be founded on the belief that you have something special to offer the world of business, commerce or the general public (why else would customers come to you rather than established companies?). The three ages of a business may be described as (1) innovative – bold new concept, (2) established – trading up – wider service/product range – profitable, and (3) conservative – top-heavy – vulnerable – declining profitability. You are at the start point, about to make your mark.

Once you are out in the marketplace, you are potentially vulnerable to other people coming along and using your ideas to promote their businesses – how can you stop this happening? Sometimes, it really is impossible to stop someone else – either because your idea is insufficiently unique or possibly because they have larger pockets. In the latter case, it helps if you know that someone else with long pockets (e.g. the Government) is on your side. This chapter summarises the main legal protections available to you and your business, but recognise too that sometimes, sheer commercial speed and being 'out there' exploiting the ideas can be a significant protection.

3.2 Your idea

The starting point for a new business is a **business idea**. Your idea may be a product or a service. You may develop the idea from your existing know-how and resources, or you may start by identifying a promising market. Of course, know-how and markets are both needed and if you have one only, you will need to acquire or develop skills and/or knowledge of the other.

Your idea may not be original. A sound idea with appropriate know-how of markets and management can be successful even it if isn't new; at least it will have a track record. An ordinary idea, well implemented and effectively marketed, is likely to be more successful than a brilliant innovation poorly introduced.

Ways in which you may be able to come up with a business idea which is not wholly original include:

Copying: seeing a product or service that works commercially, finding a market which could use it but in which it isn't available, and introducing it there. For instance, Western Europe and North America are rich sources of business ideas that are not yet available or adequately exploited outside these regions.

Franchising: which amounts to copying somebody else's business idea with their full support, in exchange for a fee.

Buying an existing business can provide a useful shortcut, but can also present possible pitfalls.

More original ideas may take the form of:

Product spin-off: think of a new use or variation of an existing product or service and set up a business to exploit it.

Personal experience: when did you last say to yourself, 'why doesn't somebody invent a ...? It would make my life easier, or solve an immediate problem?' The real entrepreneur will follow up by asking 'Why don't I ...?'

Whatever the source or nature of your business idea, if it is to succeed it must fill a market need. What is more, that market must have at least one of three characteristics:

- it should be growing (or already be large)
- it should not be very price-sensitive
- it must not already be occupied and dominated by strong competition (unless that competition is very vulnerable to new ideas).

However good your idea, remember that customers do not buy ideas, products or services. Customers have needs – real or imagined – and buy something to satisfy those needs (solutions to their problems, answers to their questions, higher sales and so on).

Put succinctly, they want **benefits not features**. Market and sell your product, service or idea accordingly.

Before proceeding any further, summarise your idea, including:

- description of the product or service
- why it will sell
- description of the proposed market
- estimate of the price you can charge
- how it will be sold (shops, sales people, distributors, mail order, internet)
- estimate of potential, initial and later sales volumes; timescales
- how it will be made, if a product, or carried out, if a service
- estimate of likely cost to you.

3.3 Protecting your business idea

Many businesses are based on a seemingly simple idea, whether this is a product or a service. Some such ideas are not original, but others represent material innovation and it may be possible to protect or secure the advantage it affords. If the basic idea is not adequately protected in law, the business **'USP'** or **unique selling proposition** may be lost and the present and future prospects of the business seriously affected. There are a number of ways in which such ideas may be protected and in almost all cases, if such protection is desired, professional assistance should be obtained. The cost of obtaining such assistance will almost always be substantially less than the losses incurred if it is not sought – or if it is sought too late.

Remember too that ideas can also be protected (during the time you are seeking formal protection, or if it cannot be obtained) by keeping them secret as long as practical.

Ideas which can be protected in some formal way are usually referred to as **Intellectual Property** and your interest therein as Intellectual Property Rights or 'IPR'.

The following notes relate to UK intellectual property rights, but similar protection can be obtained in most other industrialised countries. Detailed information on IPR protection is available at the government-backed websites **www.patent.gov.uk** and at **www.intellectual-property.gov.uk**.

3.3(a) Patents

Patent protection is probably the best known way of safe-guarding a business idea, but not everyone is familiar with the range of protection afforded, nor the extent of the protection. Very simply, patenting is a *sole monopoly right* awarded by the State to a patentee for a fairly long period, to reward the inventors for their work. It can be broadened to have international status. Patent protection is the broadest monopoly right awarded and protects the invention itself rather than the form in which the idea is expressed. If the invention to be protected has been disclosed to anyone, anywhere, it will prevent the award of a patent – no matter how good the idea.

To obtain a patent, a description of the idea to be patented must be filed with the Patent Office **prior to any public disclosure** and the idea itself must be an innovation **not seen elsewhere in the world** and one that is not obvious to a person skilled in that application. Some ideas may not be patentable – for example literary works or methods of doing business – but other IPR protections may protect them. Patents can cover products, processes, materials and formulae and can, if properly maintained, grant up to a 20-year monopoly right. Patents do not necessarily guarantee that the inventor will not infringe another patent; furthermore, patents may be challenged or ignored by others (e.g. large firms with deeper pockets) or others may invest in the development of their own products to circumvent or compete with the patent.

3.3(b) Trademarks

Most people are familiar with the concept of a trademark in the form of a product name or company name, but trademarks can comprise words or symbols or colours or even smells – or any combination of these which is capable of being represented and can distinguish goods and services. Much wider protection is now available under recent legislation. A trademark can be registered with the Trademark Registry or can be built up by a period of trading. The registration of a trademark is not easy but can provide protection for an indefinite period of time. At the time of writing, trade marks can be registered for ten years and renewed every ten years indefinitely.

There is a similar protection for providers of services and such providers may wish to seek service mark protection.

3.3(c) Copyright

Copyright arises **automatically** when an original artistic work is created (e.g. plays, books, computer programs, music) and the protection accrues to the author. The use of the © symbol is not essential in the UK, but is required (together with the date of first publication) for international protection, and serves as a warning to others of the fact of copyright protection. In establishing copyright, it is important to establish your originality of the process of creation for example and to retain good records of this, including the date.

In general terms, copyright lasts for the life of the author plus 70 years, although sound broadcasts and cable programmes are covered for 50 years.

3.3(d) Registered designs

Where the shape, aesthetic appearance, or eye appeal of an article is important to the user and/or purchaser, it is possible to register a design and be protected by this registration initially for five years, which may be extended up to a total period of 25 years. Registration of the design does not automatically entitle the owner to use the design, because a competitor could seek revocation on the grounds that the design is not new. However a registered design is relatively cheap and easy to obtain, and may afford some protection.

3.3(e) Know-how

Although there is no definitive term for what comprises 'know-how', it generally implies confidential information regarding the practical side of applying or manufacturing or working a patented invention. It is not strictly a property to be protected, but is clearly something that may be confidential and which can be protected from disclosure or which may be licensed for use.

Know-how protection is therefore not something applied for, but something protected by marking anything related to know-how as 'CONFIDENTIAL' and by restricting access. There is no specific period of protection, but it can last for many years.

3.3(f) Design right

Under the Copyright, Designs and Patents Act 1988, protection is provided for original designs for a period of up to 15 years without a requirement for registration with an authority and is not limited (as are registered designs) to the aesthetic appearance; this is called design right.

There is a series of exemptions to design right legislation based on the concept of 'must fit', to allow, for example, independent car exhaust manufacturers to make exhaust components that fit the original engine/exhaust system.

3.3(g) Passing off

Whilst there is no legal protection to be applied for, it is possible to protect the reputation of a company by challenging any competitor which 'passes off' its services as being the services of another, although commercial damage by reason of the misrepresentation must be shown or be shown to be likely.

3.3(h) Who is protected?

In general terms, the inventor of the products, applications or service is protected, but there may be occasions when professional assistance would be valuable in establishing who should get the protection, for example:

(1) If an employee invents something during the course of working for the employer, then protection accrues to the employer. If, however, it is

developed outside working hours, as part of the employee's hobby, then the employee will normally derive the benefit (unless his employment contract provides otherwise). There may be areas of business expansion which fall in between these two where clarification should be sought.

(2) Where contracts for work by sub-contractors are involved, these should specify to whom the protection accrues. If not, the protection does not automatically accrue to the inventor, nor necessarily to the person/company paying for the work to be done. For example, a consultant being requested to write a report for a client analysing a market (and containing non-confidential information) may or may not retain the copyright of the report, depending on how the contract is worded.

If your ideas are protected and you wish to offer/sell/license some use of your IPR, professional assistance in drawing up an agreement is critical to ensure that you only license the use that you intend (and can therefore license elsewhere as appropriate), that you do get paid for any use of your IPR, or no use at all, and that other eventualities are properly catered for.

3.4 Action in breach

If someone breaches your rights under one of the above protections and uses your intellectual property rights without your permission, then **prompt action** is required to:

- obtain an injunction to stop further breaches of the protection
- obtain compensation for your loss of profit or other loss
- deal with the goods created by the breach in an appropriate fashion.

In such cases, professional assistance will be required and will be expensive. It is at this stage you may discover that the cost of stopping a breach could have been substantially reduced had you taken adequate professional advice earlier.

You must, in particular, **seek professional advice before** alleging patent infringement to avoid the risk of legal action and you should seek legal advice before alleging other IPR infringement to avoid putting yourself at a distinct legal disadvantage.

3.5 Key points

- Summarise your idea – in a way that will appeal to your clients/customers.

- What protections are available to you for your idea, what do you have to do, whose help will you need, what is the likely timescale and cost?

- If patenting is possible, get very early advice, before discussing with any 'member of the public'.

- How will you best exploit your idea? By yourself/your own business, through licensing, by way of franchise, or selling it completely to a (major) company? Some other way?

- .

- .

- .

4

Marketing

4.1 Introduction

This chapter sets out to cover some aspects of marketing but it can only touch the surface of the wide range of techniques and skills needed and used. It is an area meriting much research and training – and the careful preparation of your own detailed strategies and plans. Remember too, that markets and competitors are constantly changing, new techniques and technologies emerge or new legislation can change the competitive environment. You will need to stay alert to these changes, adapt, and implement new marketing strategies and tactics.

Possibly the most common **basic reason for failure** of a business is inadequate market research, followed by poor marketing, over-ambitious plans and an inflexible approach. This, together with poor sales technique, will show up in a shortage of cash!

Before you launch your business, it's advisable to **conduct some market research** to find out whether your hunch or idea is sound and to understand better the market in which you are to operate. Do people actually want to buy the product or service you have set your heart on? The market research any new business needs to do is directed towards identifying a group of potential customers with common needs, so that the product can be tailored accordingly, the competitive products evaluated, and benefits designed into the product or service to give it a competitive edge.

Customers are the life blood of your business and the sooner you start finding out about them the better! Once you are in operation, they will still be the most significant area of your business to concern you and should remain a priority. To address this need, think through carefully the marketing options available to you, the costs and timescales of each, your preferred option, how you can implement it, and what you intend to do to capitalise on the successful outcomes!

4.2 Market research

Your first steps in marketing should be your involvement in initial market research. This is likely to be based on your own employment experience and general knowledge, aided (or constrained!) by your investigation so far and enthusiasm for the new business. You should talk with all your contacts in the relevant areas as much as possible – recognising that you may wish to retain some element of confidentiality about your proposed activity in case it should alert or stimulate competition.

You could, depending on your product/service, set up meetings with potential users to understand their needs, or set up a small market research study of the general public. If seeking views, prepare your questions carefully in advance. A 'closed' question such as 'Would you be interested in a made-to-measure shirt service?' is likely to be less informative for you than an 'open' question such as 'How often might you buy a made-to-measure shirt?' and 'What do you look for?'

Try to be as detached as possible from the business as you ask questions of your potential customers – dispassionate informative comments are your goal and you need to encourage your respondents to be open with you. It may be very tempting to argue with comments made, to explain more clearly or whatever – or to take criticism of your ideas personally. Your objective however is to learn from such comments and to test out your proposals. Seek advice from more experienced researchers on how to plan and run your research programme.

There may also be significant and helpful data already available (and free) from existing sources, such as:

- public libraries (general or specialist)
- Government statistics (see 'A Brief Guide to Sources' from the Press and Information Service, Great George Street, London, SW1P 3AP)
- Government publications – e.g. 'Business Matters', or information from the Office for National Statistics

- Department of Trade and Industry
- trade directories (e.g. Kelly's or Key British Enterprises)
- Yellow Pages
- internet research
- The Chartered Institute of Marketing.

A fuller approach to market research is of course far more comprehensive and scientific and involves the gathering of statistical and other information from many sources. You could even buy in the specialised services of a market research firm or individual expert, or published market research reports (either free or purchased).

Key information required includes establishing who your present customers are (or who the first ones are likely to be), why they (will) buy from you – the real and the stated reasons – and what other customers this might lead to. Other information includes:

- location of customers, for your retail outlets etc
- time taken by customers to commit to orders
- usual order sizes
- seasonal demands and timescales, seasonal ordering
- routes to the market (e.g. direct, via agents, distributors or installers)
- pricing points
- profitable v unprofitable business (margins, volumes, specials, 'sale' seasons, 'troublesome' customers and so on)
- competition – their perceptions of all the items listed above
- any testing required, legislative requirements
- perceived reasons for changes in demand, technical or legal issues etc.

Updating all of the above will be required regularly until you start your business – and then regularly afterwards.

Write up your findings as you go, as if you had to present a report to colleagues. To monitor changes over time, you will need to continue to research your market and the data collected can prove valuable in operating your business more effectively.

4.3 The marketing message

Once you know what your product is, why it should sell, and who you want to buy it, you can plan your approach to marketing. A number of the issues about marketing that you need to consider are set out in this chapter – which should give you the opportunity to move on later to the mode of selling.

First of all though – what is marketing?

Marketing is defined here as the process that gets you in front of a potential customer/client (or vice-versa) giving you an opportunity to sell, and a process which makes that selling easier. It is about increasing the awareness of your product or service in the marketplace in order to create opportunities for face-to-face meetings which can then be followed by active selling to convert attention or interest into a purchase, or firm orders, or a contract – which will be paid for.

This chapter summarises a range of marketing approaches and the suggestions should be developed by you depending on your service or product, on the market in which you operate, and on your individual set of skills. Where you find yourself needing extra skills, you can develop those aspects of need by (for example) referring to some of the large library of books available on marketing (and selling) or by seeking specialist training, or by engaging professional help on an employed or consultancy basis..

Any serious approach to marketing should not only entail research into the marketplace and competitive companies, services and products, but also a review of the marketing techniques of others and those recommended in books, magazines, trade journals, talks and so on, perhaps even consultations with marketing professionals. You need to be up-to-date and fluent in current jargon at all times. You are responsible for choosing the most appropriate marketing techniques for your business at any time and need to be aware of the wide range of options.

Marketing is often confused with selling and the span of marketing techniques varies enormously depending on the products or services being marketed. Selling techniques are covered in a later chapter and although marketing is different from selling, in a smaller business the distinctions between the two are not as clear-cut as in larger companies.

Your objective in seeking to carry out effective marketing and selling is to put you in a position where you are able to choose to do more work of the type you enjoy and do well – and to get paid well for it. You will need to consider the general image you need to portray and the specific information you wish to communicate. A successful marketing approach can:

- ☑ catch the attention of potential customers
- ☑ educate them in the product characteristics and the benefits it offers them
- ☑ create a purchase desire for the product
- ☑ lead potential customers to ask for the product
- ☑ improve the general reputation of your product, service or business as a whole.

4.4   Why do you need marketing?

Running a successful independent business is tough. Many people start out with great enthusiasm for their product or service only to discover the need for marketing after the business is launched and when there are insufficient sales. It is then likely to take some time (with little or no income) to create an impression in the marketplace. With no income it is also difficult to feel confident about investing in marketing. Furthermore, it may be difficult by then to abandon the intention to set up on your own and get back into the jobs market. This does not create a good environment to undertake effective marketing! **Far better to start on day one.**

Regular surveys of start-up smaller businesses reveal that most are unsuccessful – some put the failure percentages at over 90%. The main reason behind the failures is poor, or the complete absence of, marketing – although it may show up as insufficient business/sales, no cash coming in etc. Some other reasons for lack of success include:

- ☒ after initial launch and a period of activity, a tendency to wait for business to arrive
- ☒ a built-in fear of cold-calling, a necessity in self-employment (Can you consider it?)
- ☒ the wrong marketing mix
- ☒ giving the client the wrong 'signals' – e.g. by appearing desperate to 'sell' business.

☒ not knowing what to do next

☒ lack of a clearly defined service or focus.

To initiate effective and appropriate marketing, I recommend that you prepare a formal, written and systematic marketing plan, which will overcome internal and external resistances such as:

☒ other people being more active marketeers

☒ great competitive pressure

☒ your limited budget (time and funds) which needs to be allocated wisely

☒ too much business, leaving no time for marketing or planning – or no business, leading to panic marketing

☒ personal objections to (e.g.) selling or cold calling

☒ finally, preparing and implementing an effective marketing plan is hard work and the alternative of focusing on your normal business instead is almost certainly far easier! However, given normal lead times, a lack of marketing today means a lack of business in some 3 – 12 months time.

In his book *'Start and Run a Profitable Consultancy Business'*, Douglas A Gray says:

'Many consultants fail, or maintain marginal income, because of poor marketing. Consultants frequently do not appreciate the necessity of marketing, do not like to market, do not want to market or do not take time to market.'

So, what are the steps towards active and effective marketing? One approach suggests the following.

1   Analyse your product/service carefully; closely define/target the potential clients and market.

2   Consider and choose from the marketing methods available.

3   Prepare your detailed marketing plan.

4   Price your product/service.

5   Take action – to enable a move into selling mode.

These steps are considered in the following sections.

4.5   Analyse the product/service and market

If you are to market your product/service effectively, you must ensure that the benefits to the client are obvious and that you understand the reasons that customers purchase. Your marketing must be geared to both.

Review the offerings, USPs (unique selling propositions) and marketing methods of other suppliers operating in the sector and consider what could be your competitive advantages and disadvantages. Think about how other suppliers, especially those of a similar size, address the marketplace. Perhaps buy something from your main competitors and see what strengths and weaknesses they expose. You may also need to review any legal or professional issues or codes of behaviour (e.g. those allowed by your professional institute or expected by your clients). Would it benefit your marketing if you were to join a professional association such as the Chartered Institute of Marketing or the Institute of Management Consultants? This could give you more contacts by attending local and central meetings – indeed, any meetings. Be a 'joiner'!

The process of analysing the product/service to be offered may require several iterations for you to match your offering to an opportunity market. The 'end-game' is to be able to define your product/service in your literature and orally to potential customers/clients in such a way that they will easily relate to **benefits** and will 'want to buy'. In the end, with effective marketing and selling (and perhaps some luck!) you will be selling and the client/customer will be buying the same thing – the two perceptions may not be exactly the same, but the service/product supplied will be.

What causes your customers to come to you and buy?

Can you complete the sentence, 'People buy from my business because …'? This is what differentiates you from others and is key to your future and your marketing. It could be your location, the unique products/service, the quality of service, or because you are the only xxxx in the area. Or it might be your personality or particular skill (e.g. for a well-known chef). It should not be based on being the cheapest price – others can almost always beat you on this.

Having decided to specialise in a potential market, try setting down the probable **key concerns** or desires of your target clients. One way of doing this would be to prepare ten groups of 'headlines' starting with words such as:

Protect....	Grow....	Restore....	Reduce....
Develop....	Identify....	Improve....	Replace....
Restructure....	Establish....		

Use each of these ten verbs to open 5-10 statements such as 'Protect our market position as the leading supplier'. Note that at this stage **these are client concerns or desires**, not part of your offering. Then state how you would meet the needs. A later function of these 'identified concerns' is for use in networking discussions, to see if they really are the concerns/desires of potential customers..

Better early than late, you will want to set up your own **information database** covering your market niche, including client and non-client files, background market data, people who influence clients and especially identifying the buying units within a firm – indeed any data that will support your role as a leading source of knowledge. Establish procedures for updating and maintaining the information, supported by other on- and off-line commercial databases as required. Provide yourself with up-to-date sector reference material including books, trade journals, competitor brochures, trade association materials and contact lists and phone numbers.

If you record names, addresses and/or phone numbers, i.e. personal details, you will come within the provisions of the Data Protection Act and are required to register with the Information Commissioner. This can be done online, for a modest sum, at **www.dataprotection.gov.uk**. Failure to do so can have severe consequences.

Bear in mind too that having defined the service offered, when introducing it to the market, you may need to 'blur the edges' of your speciality to give yourself the opportunity to extend your offering.

Before moving on to the next section, try to draw up a brochure for your business. I'm not suggesting that you should yet (or even ever) send out or use a brochure, but in this age of junk mail, we are all used to discarding brochures which have been carefully designed and are sent to each of us as a valued potential customer on a selected mailing list. Could you now prepare a compelling A4 sheet which would persuade someone to buy from your business? Try it out on a few friends!

4.6 Choose from the available marketing methods

Many techniques and media are available to help you put your marketing message across, but all rely on your communicating through (i) creating an implication or image (ii) presenting tangible materials (graphic design and/or written) and (iii) talking about your product/services. These will be used either singly or in combination through one or a number of media. Your marketing options will involve:

(a)	Image	(b)	Advertising
(c)	Mailshots	(d)	Cold calling
(e)	PR	(f)	Networking
(g)	Linking with others	(h)	The internet
(i)	Managing your customer base		

These are dealt with briefly below.

4.6 (a) Creating/maintaining your image

Part of the process of determining the message you want to impart or imply will certainly require consideration of your business image, which has an impact on how people feel about your business. This will include the perceived quality and price, reputation and reliability, value for money and associations (e.g. fashionable, successful, desirable, patriotic etc). People buy for emotional and rational reasons and your image can influence both.

Many businesses will prepare a brochure (with matching letterheads and business cards) for mailshots or 'leave-behinds'. The brochure should describe clearly the business and the client benefits, without being too restrictive (to allow an expansion of the range or service). This may be the first (and only?) contact your potential client has with you, so you must ensure that the image created is appropriate. Practical issues like design and production costs and the ability to mail out cheaply will also require consideration. If you decide you need a brochure, you will almost certainly need professional assistance to prepare one.

What are you going to call your business – the business name? Both the 'sole trader or limited company?' decision and the business name itself are relevant. The name should, if possible, encapsulate the business (you know immediately the business of Budget Rent-a-Van). The name should have positive, not negative, connotations (does 'John Smith Associates' convey the right business image, or is it just a one man band? Does the word 'Limited' convey a more established image justifying the added cost?). Although not part of marketing, you must take professional advice at an early stage on all the implications of the sole trader versus limited company decision to ensure you position your marketing strategy correctly. There are restrictions on the names you can use – and you will need to check first that no one else is using the same name; if you are forming a limited company, this step is resolved in the process of registration with Companies House.

Depending on the requirements of your business, you may not need to rent premises on day one, but the environment must be a suitable one in which to work – and convey the desired image to clients who telephone or visit – whether you have invited them to visit or not. (Location is important for most businesses, and particularly for retail organisations, and this is dealt with in Chapter 13, section 13.3 – see how it applies to you.). If working from home, set aside an area where you can work uninterrupted and which is 'your office'. Separate phone and fax lines (or broadband for the same effect) are desirable and these days a computer is almost essential for reports and letters, sending and receiving email, online market research, setting up and running a website, and possibly for accounting, order processing, and other automated processes. Your business image also includes what you wear and the car you drive – neither too flashy/expensive nor too 'interesting'/unsuccessful – how the telephone is answered and customer enquiries dealt with, your business stationery and marketing material, how your product is packaged (if applicable) or service delivered, and your website (if you have one).

4.6(b) Advertising

Advertising is generally expensive, but can be used selectively by smaller, newer businesses as part of a marketing campaign. It may be appropriate to advertise in specialist literature or directories, or at specialist exhibitions, but expensive advertising as such is not widely used by smaller firms. Direct feedback on the effectiveness of advertising is difficult to obtain in any sector (remember the old saying that *'50% of advertising is wasted – the trouble is knowing which 50%'*). This seems especially so with smaller businesses. However, it can be used boldly, imaginatively and expensively e.g. for a marketing consultancy to gain wide publicity, but must be followed up quickly and well.

Bearing in mind this is an expensive option, you must be certain that your advertisement is going to stand a reasonable chance of being read by the relevant decision makers. This usually means advertising in specific professional, trade or industry publications. Understand too your target area – if your sales are to people living within a 30 minute drive, it does not pay to advertise nationally (unless it is part of a specific business expansion plan).

Inclusion in specific directories, both reference and telephone, under one or more classifications should be closely considered. Make it easy for potential customers to contact you. If your target area is the private client or local consumer, local and 'free copy' newspapers should be a consideration of any advertising programme, possibly even the local post-office or newspaper shop (see the comments below on PR to support your advertising).

An advertisement should be eye-catching without being brash or controversial and should briefly outline the product, stressing the main benefits strongly. Never hint at or reveal the price. National advertising is usually out of the question unless a high initial income makes it a feasible proposition in your cash flow projection.

Local radio may be interested in talks or interviews; make sure questions are pre-agreed and fully discussed prior to your air-time. This 'free' PR will then complement and support the paid-for radio advertising.

Advertising takes time to be effective and one insertion is unlikely to achieve a sale. You will probably need to consider a long term advertising campaign to build awareness over a period.

4.6(c) Mail shots

Direct mail works better for some businesses than others and before investing heavily, you may want to assess how appropriate it is for you. Realise that your mail shot may now be someone else's 'junk mail'. There is no guarantee that it will ever be read or even be received by your targeted person. Anything less than a really compelling letter with an 'attention grabber' in the first line in unlikely to succeed – so take time to prepare and get relevant assistance. How many/much do you have to sell to pay for the mailing? A £100 mail shot standing a good chance of creating regular gross margin of £1,000 is a better bet than a mail shot costing £1,000 with potential to create unit sales of £5.

It is essential that you research your target individual/company customer carefully and that you have the correct name of your targeted person. Neither printing nor post is cheap, so mailing the average brochure (a simple A4 two-fold, two-colour sheet) plus postage and envelope could cost between 80p – 150p per set, more if your brochure contains more than two colours. Remember too that mailings may need to be repeated several times over a 3-12 month period to be effective at the time purchase decisions are made. Target your mail shots as carefully as possible and maintain comprehensive records to enable you to assess over time what works and what does not work – and how long each variety takes to turn into an enquiry or better still a sale. Remember mail shots that only generate enquiries end up costing you twice as much as those that get no response at all. You pay out once to send out the mailing and again to deal with the enquiry that goes no-where! It is therefore important to 'convert' as many enquiries as possible into actual sales.

Response from mail shots is low, e.g. in the well-researched area of mail order selling, response generally runs at about 0.75% to 2%, and conversion of these leads into sales is perhaps between 5% and 15%. Make it easy for your targets to contact you. Include your phone number, email address, web address and post address. It may be appropriate to include a reply paid or Freepost response card to make it easier still for potential customers to respond. Your hard-earned responses represent real selling opportunities, so a follow-up telephone call within 7 days is essential to seek to improve the odds – which is only possible on small targeted mail shots. When you call, don't try to sell or discuss your brochure – concentrate on trying to arrange a meeting, because selling is usually a face-to-face operation.

Finally try to batch your mail shots (and send a limited number at a time) in as close a geographical area as possible – any meetings can then be arranged on a cost-effective schedule.

4.6(d) Cold Calling

Cold calling is possibly the least effective way to approach potential customers and should be replaced or preceded by any other approach if at all possible to improve your effectiveness. However, cold approaches may be required at some stage and should be directed at selected lists of target customers. These lists should be developed from your personal telephone/address book and business cards, from guest lists of functions you have attended, from lists purchased from specialist suppliers, from professional institutes, from research by you in trade publications in reference libraries such as Kelly's directory or Dun & Bradstreet, or through the assistance of direct mail research firms listed in the Direct Mail Directory, British Rate and Data ('BRAD') etc. You may also be able to combine your mailing with other vendors to reduce your costs. (NB Data Protection registration – see section 4.5)

Cold approaches by telephone are expensive in time – time probably better spent on planning and implementing a controlled mailshot, which can then be followed up by phone. However, if you do plan to cold call by phone, remember that very definite telephone selling skills are required (try **never to cold call physically**, i.e. knocking on doors unexpectedly – success rates are low and costs are high). To be effective, your introduction must be clear and concise and you need immediately to attract attention and interest. Your time is very short before any such interest wanes. Questions should be designed to produce the answer 'yes' – your objective must be to arrange an early meeting. **Do not try to sell your product or service over the telephone** – in nearly all cases, it just does not work.

If you are thinking about using email for cold-calling, remember that such contacts over the internet are now regulated (since October 2003) by anti-spam legislation, which requires either that there is a commercial relationship already existing between the parties, or that the email recipient has given prior consent to be contacted. Such legislation is increasingly being introduced around the world.

Pre-plan your questions and script out answers to the client's potential replies and comments. Try out your skills on a friend. Monitor your success and alter your script to improve your results. Consider specific training.

4.6(e) PR

The option of appointing a PR firm is probably too expensive initially, but do not ignore the use of PR. Although it can be a 'slow burn' and takes time and effort to generate, it is a very valuable marketing tool. Be your own PR agent, remembering that journalists have a job to do, bringing interesting and newsworthy information (not necessarily news or information about you) to their readers. Target your audience (both consumers and journalists) and make your press releases short, interesting, and newsworthy. If possible, offer something free! Try writing letters or articles for local or specialised press, charity sponsorship (coupled with newspaper coverage), offering prizes, speaking at local meetings, joining committees and so on.

Local press and radio often want features for the local business community, which you could write/prepare. Trade journals can be very approachable with articles you write for publication (on the 'hot topics') – all of which helps establish your reputation and builds your business profile. Can you address meetings of local clubs or institute branches, run committees, present awards, join societies, comment on current business issues in your market sector? What is your angle? How can you attract attention, and how should you present? Talk to the journalists and understand their 'hot buttons' of the moment (you are selling them the service of information provision!) and make your contribution topical, interesting and newsworthy.

What about initiating independent market research in the sector, which allows you to approach the target executives for their advice, comment, opinions etc on industry trends – you might even get it published, or sold! This would require a thorough and professional approach to market research, which could mean that you need to seek outside assistance.

Any PR you generate can be used in subsequent mail shots or attached to letters to former (or potential) clients. Speeches you make can perhaps be turned into articles, articles into mail shots etc. Consider all possible avenues that generate publicity for you, preferably avenues that you enjoy. As an absolute minimum, practise your enthusiastic advertisement of your product/service on your contacts.

4.6(f) Networking

Networking is the process of gaining access to potential clients and customers through people you know or through their referrals. It is the process of discussing your plans, industry trends and so on with people you know to gain further useful knowledge, more contacts, or even sales leads. There will be a surprising number of people who know you or who know of you. You must now get this network working for you. Don't actively 'sell' your products/services to them; do actively sell yourself, to confirm their belief that you are someone worth remembering and recommending to others needing assistance. What you are seeking is their active assistance in promoting you or introducing you to others and this may well entail your promoting their services in return. Ideally you will be targeting for the majority of your business to come from networking or through referrals, because of the shorter lead times and the higher conversion rates that you will be able to achieve.

The value of **networking your contacts is vital**. When running your 'own-business', you are its mouthpiece at all times and in all places. This applies to both business and social gatherings – people are always interested if you are 'doing your own thing' and you may be called on to give a presentation at a moment's notice.

Whether you are looking for consultancy assignments, agencies, a franchise, or customers for direct sales, you need to:

- start by creating a list of anyone who could or might be helpful
- plan your approach carefully – based on doing market research, sharing information, social interests etc – NOT hard selling
- follow up to see where and to whom these contacts lead you
- prepare and circulate a simple brochure which explains concisely who you are and what you have to offer
- always carry your business card and your brochure, plus samples if possible
- take every opportunity to look for new leads and draw new names from existing contacts.

Remember – effective networking can cut the time spent on marketing so that a greater proportion of the working week is spent *earning*.

Meet your contacts (regularly) to discuss the key business issues currently being addressed, news in the sector, current and recent legislation and suchlike. Test out (some of) your ideas about the market; what do your contacts see as key questions or concerns; can they be extended or improved? Recommendations from contacts make the first meeting with sales 'prospects' that much easier and allow you to move them through the 'prospect' category to problem identification and on to agreeing the contract/project at a faster rate than you could with a 'cold approach' client.

Approach satisfied clients for referrals and references – they will understand your need to develop your business – and ask for something written which you may quote. Keep old clients warm and always be on the lookout for extension business with them. They are your best prospects and it is widely considered that it costs between five and nine times as much to gain a new client as to retain an existing one. Draw their attention to any new developments in their market – they may possibly have seen them already, but will be flattered by your interest.

And finally, don't expect immediate results from your networking. In my view, what 'goes around, comes around' is a better philosophy, If you network widely, seeking to bring people together, offer solutions and advice, or contacts which may be useful, genuinely and generously helping others, it won't be long before it all starts to come back to you.

4.6(g) Linking with others

One of the options open to you is to join your marketing efforts with those of other businesses that see benefits coming to their business as a result of cooperating in your marketing – either directly or indirectly. This could be because you sell complementary products, you are located close together, or you have similar target markets for other reasons.

Such cooperation may require you to co-host joint events, mailings, speaking engagements, etc. You will need to decide which are appropriate to you and how relevant. The object of the activity for you is still to **create awareness of your own products or services** to allow direct marketing and selling by you later. The purpose of the event may be quite different and the other business's purposes are almost certainly different.

Although you can reduce your marketing costs by sharing with others, remember that they will seek to sell their services or products first. If there are budget restrictions, you may arrive at the client's door too late – or not at all.

4.6(h) The internet

The internet has become an easily accessible tool for any business to use to market and/or sell its products or services. You do not have to be large, technical, or even be a local supplier to compete over the internet. Possibly the most important thing to remember is that many of the rules of marketing still apply to the internet. Customers still have expressed and hidden needs, their attention must be attracted quickly, and they are inundated with other providers. The net itself is growing daily and it becomes more and more difficult for customers to sift out the 'junk mail'.

If you want to email customers or potential customers, rather than be accused of 'spamming', seek their sign-on approval or subscription to send them information and make it easy for them to un-subscribe (see comments under section 4.6(d) on spamming). Emails, e-newsletters or e-zines can be a great way to spread the message about your business but it still needs just as much care as 'normal' marketing. Yes, it's easy to email hundreds or people, but customers all see themselves as an individuals and your marketing should reflect this as far as you can.

If you are including the internet in your marketing plan, you will want to develop a website and also consider how to encourage people to visit it. Get professional help in its development. There are many packages that allow you to develop your site by yourself, but review other sites and see what attracts you, retains your interest, and encourages you to return. Think carefully about whom you are attracting, what they want to see, and how you will present it. Your site does not (initially at least) need to be your shop-front for selling – it can be just for bringing in the customers. Remember too that you will need to conform to the growing legislation governing use of the internet for selling.

4.6(i) Managing your customer base

You may be fortunate enough to start off with existing customers; if not, you will have to acquire new ones to get your business off the ground. Whatever happens, you will need to gain new customers. They can be found through:

- existing contacts and leads
- introductions from existing customers
- research on potential customers

- effective marketing
- effective selling.

Your business will benefit from good administration systems, which will involve maintaining records of potential and existing customers, how they were originally contacted, the response, timings and a routine for following them up (NB Data Protection registration notes Section 4.5). You will always be on the lookout for new customers as your business grows and develops. Servicing existing customers is the most rewarding market however, and they should be cultivated so that they come back for more, to buy larger quantities more often, to buy other products or services in your range and, most importantly, to act as reference sites, referrals and recommendations for new customers.

Research has shown that most customers are lost because the vendor is seen to lose interest, i.e. does not follow-up or does not keep in touch, and the customer then goes elsewhere. Maintaining your customer base is a key part of developing your business as it enables you to gear your marketing to meet actual customer needs. In most cases, it is also radically cheaper to retain or sell again to an existing customer than to identify and sell to a new one.

4.7 Prepare the marketing plan

Having considered the available marketing techniques and then having identified those which you believe are most appropriate for your business, you must prepare a marketing plan to determine what you intend to do, when you wish to implement, and how much you are going to spend (or do) to achieve what level of results. To create your plan, you will first need to identify what business the marketing activity needs to initiate. The key benchmark will be the sales you must generate in a year, which you will need to relate to a shorter timescale e.g. the average sale size, and unit sale pricing, or the average daily sales and gross margin. This enables you to tackle other issues viz:

1   Sales needed = total business costs + required personal earnings.
2   Sales needed / average sale price = number of sales required.

3   Unit sale size = days taken x daily rate (e.g. for consultancy/ professional services).
4   Daily or hourly charge-out rate = sales needed/number of working days or working hours in a year, e.g. $\dfrac{\text{sales needed}}{\text{no of working days/hours}}$

or

1   Sales needed = total business costs + total purchase costs + required personal earnings.
2   Unit gross margin = sales price – purchase cost price.
3   Total gross margin = total sales – total purchase costs.
4   Daily sales needed = sales needed or number of operating days.

At this stage, you need to make 'best guesses' for desired earnings, operating costs of running the business, gross margins, and planned marketing costs, in order to get your marketing plan started. You may also need to 'best guess' other items such as average project size on which you are likely to work, in order to define the number of projects you need to win. You can then see whether your business can afford your marketing plan and whether it is likely to generate sufficient business for you to afford to implement the marketing suggestions, e.g.:

If your desired salary as a consultant is £35,000 and estimated overheads are £10,000, then at a daily charge-out rate of £250, 10 new contracts of £4500 (or 18 working days each) are required per year for your business. At a 40% conversion rate (from quote to order), this would require you to quote for 25 assignments, which at a 20% conversion rate (from enquiry to quote) would mean that the business would need to receive 125 enquiries, which at a response rate of 1% (reasonable for a mailing) would need 12,500 targeted mailshots. At £1.50 per mailing (post, printing etc), this shows that as your marketing budget (of £18,750) now exceeds total overheads; you must change your approach and tactics or allow an increase in overheads requiring better conversion rates, higher fees or higher utilisation.

You must decide the amount to allocate to the marketing budget. To be effective, the budget is likely to be between 5% and 15% of your billings, but you will need to judge the effectiveness of the plans chosen as well as the costs. Don't spend the budget without thinking it through at least twice.

The marketing plan will need to specify what actions you take, when and to what timescales, in which areas and the expected results, and you will need to set up an effective administration system in order for you to monitor the effectiveness of each course of action undertaken. The plan needs to be robust and have your commitment – to keep you on track in the bad times (and there are always some bad times!).

Consider the options for marketing your business, some of which are outlined above, and set out the combination that you believe will be the most effective. This will require analysis of each method and its likely results, together with any combination of effects of two or more such methods (e.g. a mailshot following an article in a local paper). Estimate the costs and then compare with the overall budget for costs and sales. Without doubt you will need several assessments of the possibilities before you can settle on the marketing plan you believe will be the most effective for you – and which you can afford.

It is essential that you set targets for the business to be generated by your marketing and that you are able to track back to see how effective your marketing is. You will need to be able to cut out ineffective marketing and expand those avenues that 'deliver the goods'. Don't expect your marketing mix to stay constant over time.

4.8 Pricing your products/services

Some industries/markets are able to bear much more complex pricing structures than others, so study the competition carefully and don't be too proud to copy workable techniques. You will need to consider the pricing of your product or service at an early stage, in order to test the market. This does not mean you necessarily need to finalise pricing, but you will need to start with a rough idea of price.

Your approach to pricing may depend on many things. The acid test of nerve, of character, of self confidence, and finally of simple selling ability is seeking to persuade someone to part with their money on your terms for your goods/services and still be happy. Consider too what your product/service is worth to the customer – which could be substantially different from your costs.

You will need to consider several approaches to setting your prices or charge-out rates, but essentially prices should be as high as the market will bear. Setting prices too low could lose you as much business as setting them too high. There are two main considerations for you to bear in mind – what it costs you to provide the goods/services, and what price the market will bear (including the effects of competition or alternatives, and the value perceived by your customers).

As a generality, my advice is to price higher rather than lower.

This is because:

- it leaves room for manoeuvre and discounting
- inflation works against you, especially if you need to set a long-term 'catalogue price'
- in the event of a market downturn, the low pricer has no way to turn
- raising prices will create more difficulties than having fixed a high initial rate
- for a smaller business certainly, low price is not a strong force for customer retention.

You should also consider whether your own pricing structure will ultimately satisfy your ambitions in your chosen field. If you believe that you have good reasons for starting at a discounted price, you should certainly set yourself a time limit for becoming established or recognised, or you will never achieve the necessary margin and income. As a general rule, you should not offer 'freebies' or reduced prices, as it makes it difficult to revert to full price later. If you feel you need to start on this basis, see what extra benefits or trade-offs you can seek from the customer – such as bringing in another customer or perhaps the customer providing references for you to use with other customers or clients.

In a trading situation, you will have researched the competition, their products and the price that you believe the market will stand, as well as understanding fully your own cost structure and the basis on which you want to work. Profitability then becomes a question of containing your purchase and/or manufacturing costs, being able to sell an adequate volume to cover all the overheads, and still leave a balance sufficient to provide you with the sought-for rate of return. Your Business Plan should evaluate various options to ensure that your pricing policy sets you on the right track.

If you are a consultant or freelance, the sums are less complex and you will set a daily or hourly rate wherever possible which achieves the same objectives. In practice, the key to success will be whether you are able to charge the budgeted number of hours at the budgeted rate for each month that you planned to work – remembering that up to 50% of your time may need to be allocated to (unpaid) sales, marketing, and administration activities. This means a utilisation of 50-60% is to be expected, so to earn £200 per day in a five-day week means charging about £350 per billed day (although long term assignments may show a higher utilisation and justify lower rates).

Remember – you must have management information each month to show whether your pricing policy is working through as anticipated, or whether trading losses and unrecovered hours are gaining the upper hand. Be ready to allocate a certain amount of time to checking the progress of the business year and to reviewing the pricing policy at the appropriate time. Understand the value that customers place on quality and personal service in your business.

In assessing your costs, remember that some costs (rent, salary) will be approximately constant whatever business you do, but others (materials/ goods purchased, delivery) will vary roughly in line with sale quantities. To review competitor costs, pretend to be a buyer and ring/call in and ask! It may be appropriate in your business to apply a 'normal' mark-up on the purchase price; if so, work out how many/much you have to sell to meet your total business costs. As a generalisation – the higher the price you charge, the more you can and need to deliver in terms of (any of or all of the following) level/quality of service, convenience, extras, brand/fashion etc.

Another related aspect to consider is payment terms, for example think about the decision points you will offer the client – will you require your clients/customers to give you a deposit (25% or 33% or 50%) up-front, or make total payment? Is payment to be against invoice, statement, within 14 or 28 days of invoice/statement or make scheduled payments monthly? What about regular payment by standing order or direct debit? Should you define your Terms of Business in detail and/or in writing? Some written

Terms and Conditions are advisable for professionalism and clarity, and in case things go wrong, and this subject is addressed in Chapter 11.

4.9 Action

The previous sections should have helped you to define your marketing plans; now you can move into the implementation phase. Implement your plans to a schedule and make sure that you record what you do, and when, and using what materials, all in sufficient detail to be able to track back to any required information. You will need to measure the response resulting from each phase of your work, and the timescales of that response, in order to provide feedback to help improve performance in future. (You will be familiar with mailshots which ask you to reply to 'Dept XY' or which have a coding such as 'ST46' – these enable the advertiser to measure the response to each mailshot.)

It should go without saying that regular checking of the results achieved and a comparison with plan is essential. Check the responses generated by different types of letter by using different codes. Records must be detailed enough for you to be able to follow through from the initial mailing to the order or contract and payment.

And remember, action precedes results! You need to have a marketing plan to ensure that you do take action, every day, to market the business. It can be quite demotivating to be actively marketing your new business, with no results coming in. This is to be expected and, whilst all businesses are different, it could be anything from 3-9 months after you (e.g.) send out your first mailing that you get your first responses – and maybe you have had several follow-up mailings and phone calls since. Think of it in terms of climbing a mountain; climbing the first ridge, to the second, and so on until you reach the summit. Much the same with each client – you do not know how long each is going to take to convert to a sale. But each contact takes you a little bit closer. We all tend to take the first 'no' as a personal rejection; it is not, it just means 'no, not just now' and may mean 'Call again in a couple of weeks' time'. Activity will generate results.

4.10 Training

Many people move from employment into their 'own-business' with no training other than the subsequent 'on-the-job' experience. The skills required in the new business usually include some new skills to learn, which, if taking up a major franchise for the same business, would be included in induction training over some months. Consider whether it would be worthwhile investing in a short training course to correct or minimise identified weaknesses (such as selling or marketing). Alternatively, use a consultant or staff to fill the skills gap. At the most basic, these courses can cost around £100 and the cost of training may be distinctly less than cost of the time and effort invested in trying and failing to perform on a self-taught basis.

Having launched your business, you will need to allocate time to the maintenance and improvement of your current skills and the development of new areas of expertise. Your marketing plan should also identify (for you) how you will keep your skills up-to-date, and your time allocation must put aside, say, 10 days per year for your own training and development.

4.11 Key points

☛ Define your product or service, on paper and orally, to clients in a way that sells benefits not features. Practice your delivery. It's benefits to the client that win business.

☛ Research your customers, market and competition well before you start, to understand them fully.

☛ Research the available marketing processes (brochures, literature, mailings, PR, networking etc) to get you in front of decision-makers. Choose a working mix and implement it well. Monitor results and stay flexible.

☛ Prepare detailed marketing plans, which you can and will implement.

- Concentrate on network contacts who can recommend you, or on others who can speed up the client/customer conversion process.

- Set your prices higher rather than lower.

- Train continuously to improve and develop skills – to remain at the leading edge of (or at least up with) the industry. Read trade or professional journals regularly and thoroughly.

- See it from the client's side of the desk. It looks different from over there!

- It's not enough to be good; you need to outclass the competition.

- .

- .

- .

5

Money

5.1 Introduction

The quotation 'Love of money is the root of all evil' is often shortened to 'Money is the root of all evil'. However, money is certainly involved in and behind every business and the lack of it is put down by many as the cause of their failure. This may be the final outcome, but it is usually not the prime cause. Simply put, good businesses don't lack money. Banks don't refuse to lend. Banks are in business to lend to **soundly-based, well-managed, trustworthy businesses**. All money has a cost – banks are after all, money shops, and neither the cheapest nor the most expensive money is necessarily the best. It is likely that money will play a larger part in your life once you have your 'own-business', so time spent understanding it and its market will be well spent.

5.2 Funding the business

To consider your 'own-business' venture adequately, you will need to prepare and develop a financial section of your business plan to show how much funding is needed and if external funding is necessary. If it is clear that you need some external capital, then it could be wise to try to make arrangements for a greater amount than your first plan suggests. Is your plan conservative or bold? What further finance might you need? In what circumstances? Are there sufficient contingencies in the plan?

In working out your plan, provide sufficiently for the start-up costs of the business – these are usually much greater than anticipated – it's a new area about which you may know little. If you under-estimate your needs, there is nothing worse than having to go back, cap in hand, for further funding, trying to explain why the original figures were optimistic – at a time when your business may seem much less attractive to a lender or investor. It may be possible to borrow the funds arranged in stages up to the maximum agreed, with the proviso that the later stages of financing do not all have to be taken immediately (or perhaps they need never be taken up); this could reduce your interest costs.

Having determined how much funding is likely to be required, the next step is to decide the appropriate source. For example, consider:

- existing personal savings etc.
- by increasing your house mortgage, perhaps with a second charge
- bank loan
- family finance, friends or business associates, or 'Business/Venture Angels'
- specialist finance, venture/development capital, etc.

Most of these options are fairly well-known – but 'angels' are people who will invest in businesses personally, usually ones operating in a sector they understand, and in which they will want to take some management role (possibly as an active, but non-executive, director). If taking the venture/development capital route, you should ask for recommendations and assistance from your professional advisors. It is worth bearing the following points in mind when going into the market for such specialist investment finance.

- You will certainly require a business plan – not just cash flow and profit projections.
- If possible, obtain competitive quotations at any level.
- Involve your professional advisor.
- You will be able to borrow more cheaply if you offer good security.
- You will almost certainly need to offer some equity in your business for larger and more specialised deals e.g. from venture or development capital sources.

5.3 Getting bank funding

The major banks spend large sums of money in order to attract accounts of both new and existing businesses and:

- advertise extensively on television, on radio, and in the national press
- produce high quality brochures aimed at the small business proprietor, often having special packs for start-up businesses.

If you intend approaching a bank for overdraft/loan facilities you will need to satisfy the manager on several points (in order of importance).

Type of business – Some businesses are more attractive than others for the bank, especially for start-ups or early stage firms. You may find one bank more receptive than another.

Person – You are the type of person who should be helped, e.g. you have a satisfactory record of credit worthiness (i.e. you have borrowed and repaid), you have 'done your homework' and you have researched the business idea.

Amount – You know exactly how much you need to borrow (evidenced by cash forecasts in the business plan) and are introducing funds of your own.

Repayment – The business can produce sufficient profit to pay you a 'living wage' and, more importantly, repay the loan/overdraft. Have you allowed for repayments in the business plan as well as for interest and bank charges?

Security – You have the collateral available to secure the borrowing. Remember, **banks will not hesitate to retrieve the security** if you do not honour your side of the agreement!

There are other matters the manager will be considering.

Expediency – Whether there are valuable 'family' connections at the bank that may influence the bank's decision.

Rates – What rate of interest is to be payable – usually a percentage above the rate at which the bank borrows itself (Base Rate). This Base Rate can vary and you must be prepared for it to go up as well as down. Commission (bank charges plus an arrangement fee) is also negotiable. Be prepared to compare rates with competitor banks as total rates can vary widely. Remember too that overdraft interest rates are substantially greater than for term loans and that overdrafts are repayable immediately on **demand by the bank**.

Services – The banks make substantial profits from selling pensions, insurance, mortgages and so on and will attempt to sell you such services when agreeing facilities. Remember to compare these products with those provided by competitors before signing on the dotted line.

Even bank managers are targeted and paid salary increases and bonuses according to their level of success.

Remember too that banks are conservative institutions. Particularly, they do not like surprises! So try to keep your bank manager/official informed about your business – even when it is going through difficult times – although you do need to keep in mind that the manager's loyalty is to the bank and not to the customer (you). So if trouble is really brewing, the bank manager will take whatever action is necessary to protect the bank. When you hear a businessman saying something like, 'The bank pulled the rug/withdrew support' the likelihood is that the bank was not fully aware of the problems, was not told of realistic solutions, or was otherwise 'suddenly surprised'. Your bank should feel like a supportive business – keep it in touch.

5.4 Grants

The idea of receiving a grant sounds attractive. In practice, it may not be quite so easy to get one, as the only grant available may be to cover the period before business income is generated and there may be preconditions. The grant provider will have other objectives such as employment creation and/or area regeneration and there may be competition for the grants. Obtain details in good time from the grant provider of any requirements it may have for applicants. There may also be grants available from the European Community budget – there are organisations that will help you to find the most appropriate source and grant, often on a 'profit-sharing' basis. Grants can prove unduly expensive in time and effort to obtain.

From time to time there may be special Government grants, e.g. for assisted areas of the country or for the unemployed. Sometimes these are operated on different bases around the country. You should enquire about such schemes **before** starting out in business in case that is a precondition of the assistance that your application is made before start-up. You may also find that funding is only to be provided on a matched basis, i.e. the grant-provider will invest the same amount as you do. Be careful about engaging grant-finders who charge an up-front fee. Usually, when advising my clients, I'll suggest that they are often better off not to seek grant aid. For more information, see 'Grants' in Appendix VI.

5.5 Other sources

Other forms of funding from banks include factoring, hire purchase, and leasing. Factoring or invoice discounting is a way of borrowing up to 80% of the cash due from as-yet-unpaid invoices, in exchange for interest and a fee. This is a valuable source of funding for many newer businesses, even though it is often more expensive than normal bank borrowings (but these may not be available) and may be difficult to replace in due course with other forms of finance. Factoring is probably more attractive for the expanding (rather than stable state) business. It is certainly worth considering.

You can approach family and personal friends, but this requires care for a number of reasons. Firstly, you must make it clear to your friends that they could lose their cash – even though you are sure this is unlikely. If they do lose out, they may (rightly!) hold you responsible. Show them your plans and give them time to think about it. Write out (with professional help) the basis of their investment. If you wish to seek private finance more widely, perhaps by circulating an investment proposal, **you MUST seek legal advice** as this approach will almost certainly be controlled by strict legislation, with dire penalties for non-observance.

Capital assets or equipment may be funded by hire purchase or lease finance, where the costs of purchase are spread over a long period and where ownership of the asset may or may not eventually transfer to your business. This is an area for specific advice, probably from your accountant, as tax allowances for you and/or the finance provider may make one form of such finance more viable than another. You may also benefit from special finance deals from the vendor, e.g. 0% finance.

After long periods of running other people's businesses, I have identified five other principal sources of funding often overlooked by those starting their 'own-business'.

1   Customers. Better selling prices, payment in advance, bulk orders etc all provide additional funding for you as the supplier. Could they assist in your business?
2   More efficient operations – reduced costs of running the business or better methods.
3   Tough, but fair, purchasing decisions.
4   Negotiation – on everything!
5   Not spending on overheads or non-vital costs. Not buying new – sometimes really excellent kit can be purchased second-hand – from businesses that have ceased to trade, from finance houses (equipment that they previously leased), or from private vendors (e.g. for that company car). Question every purchase – is there a cheaper alternative that fits the bill? Do you really need that size, that quality, that expensive [whatever it is]?

5.6   Money management

In setting up your 'own-business', you will need to set up business bank accounts. Most advisors will join me in recommending that you set up totally separate bank accounts for your business. You will need to keep everything separate to make it easier for you (and others) to follow the financial steps of the business you generate. You may be investigated, e.g. by HM Revenue and Customs Department ('Revenue and Customs') or other authorities, and could need to 'hand over the books' – so keep them separate. I would go further and suggest that you even consider using a different bank from your personal accounts – just to make the separation absolutely clear – one bank for the business and another bank for your personal and private accounts. Having accounts at more than one bank may also increase your chances of being able to borrow and to get the best deal.

In terms of money management, one very good suggestion (for which I claim no originality) is to have savings accounts for any periodic payments such as tax and VAT. On a weekly or monthly basis (depending on the business) work out roughly how much of your income 'belongs' to these collectors and on the same weekly or monthly basis put that percentage of your income into the savings account. Tax and VAT could account for 40%+ of your receipts, so put that much into savings – and perhaps get a pleasant surprise at the year-end when you find out that what is actually due is less than you have banked, rather than panic to find a relatively huge sum of due tax or VAT at that time.

One thing I am very keen on is the idea of generating a 'war chest' or 'fighting fund' – by which I mean having something put by for the lean times, for the bad year(s), for that recession you had not expected or just to give you time to regroup or replan. Indeed, it may be a good idea to hold off starting your business until you have built up a start-up fund that is planned to carry you through the first problem period. I agree that you do have to be adventurous, but a degree of caution is needed as well.

Later in the book I will deal with accounting for your progress – but it goes almost without saying that you will need to know where your business finances are on a very regular basis to know if you are surviving and growing – or not.

5.7 Key points

- Money is important to your business! Buy the best – for you, and use it wisely.

- Understand what banks and finance houses want before you approach them.

- Consider all the relevant forms of finance – including 'hidden' options like not spending or operating more efficiently.

- There is always money available – for well-run, profitable businesses. How can your business be attractive to the money-men?

- .

- .

- .

6

Forming the Business – the Legal Issues

6.1 Introduction

In deciding to set up in business on your own, one of the practical issues you will need to address will be the legal form that you actually set up for the business. There are a number of options from which to choose, but most commonly, one of four main ways are used to operate a business:-

- Sole trader
- Partnership
- Limited company (public or private)
- Limited liability partnership

Whilst there are often no clear-cut reasons for choosing one form against the others, there are several key areas to be considered. Different advisors will often place different priorities on each of these (for example, accountants may favour the most effective tax vehicle) and whilst some criteria can be fairly objective, others are of a more emotional nature; this applies both to your view of the business and the marketplace, and to your assessment of how the marketplace sees you and your business.

Whatever form you decide on, it can be changed at a later date albeit at some cost, the net cost depending on the change made. There are different rules governing the operation of each form of business and it is most important that you take early professional advice from your accountant and/or lawyer in establishing your business. At an early stage it will also be useful to gain advice from the library of advisory books and from your friends and contacts. The basic 'rules' and some of the key issues to consider are set out below.

6.2 The basic relevant rules

6.2(a) Sole trader

This is the simplest and probably the **most flexible** form of trading and, after considering your options, if you have no clear indication of another route, it is probably the way you should start in business. Someone starting up in business on their own is most often recommended to do so as a sole trader. It is the **simplest to establish**, gives most scope for speedy and effective decisions, has least formalities, and can most cheaply be dismantled if, for whatever reasons, you have second thoughts. A sole proprietor can introduce and withdraw money from the business with little formality and with no Income Tax or National Insurance ('NI') implications.

You can, of course, employ people on your own terms (e.g. salaried, profit share, sub-contractor or consultant) and remain a sole trader – the rest of the income is yours. The downside is the risk of failure, in which case **creditors can proceed against your private estate** almost to your last penny. If you are declared bankrupt, you will face restrictions on your future personal and trading activities.

If you start trading as a sole trader, you must tell Revenue and Customs promptly (ranging from immediately to within several months, depending on the issue). Similar timescales apply to any start-up route. You should discuss the timing and content of your letter to do this with your accountant.

You must also check whether you are obliged to register for VAT, i.e. if your projected sales exceed the annual limit (e.g. set at £60,000 from 1 April 2005, following the March 2005 Budget); if not, do you want to register anyway?

If you are trading under a name other than your own (even if John Smith trades as John Smith Antiques), you must include your own name on your key business stationery (invoices, letterhead) to identify that the business is a sole trader. You must also include an address for valid service of documents – and display all the same information clearly on business premises.

The accounts for a sole trader are simple, as are the requirements to file information. However, you are personally responsible for all the business debts and (if you need them) you are eligible for lower social security benefits.

6.2(b) Partnership

If more than one person is involved in the start-up of a business, it may be appropriate to enter into a partnership. Although a separate legal structure, Tax and NI apply broadly as for a sole trader and you have the **benefits of shared responsibilities and additional skills** and resources. As with sole trading, there is no protection for your private estate in the event of the business failing and there is no way to avoid the 'joint and several liability' you bear for business debts, even if they were caused by (an)other partner(s).

Whilst not legally required, I believe it is vital for you to draw up a **partnership agreement** and strongly recommend that you instruct a solicitor to do this. The partnership agreement or deed could cover (inter alia) the objectives of the business and growth/ownership plans, who invests what, the shares of profits, effects of different investment or hours put into the business, drawings before year end, absences, who does what, partners leaving or joining the firm etc. Also, note the following.

- In any partnership, the partners are **'jointly and severally' responsible for all debts** and obligations of the partnership. This means that another partner could incur business debts that could require you to sell all your personal assets to meet the debt even where you may not have agreed to the actions. Be sure you can trust your partners!

- A sleeping partner in a business may take no management role, but is still responsible for the partnership debts.

- If one partner leaves or another partner joins, in general terms, one partnership ends and a new partnership begins. However, partnerships can be deemed to be continuous if it is advantageous to do so and all partners agree. This can still be useful for tax planning, but if your partner changes his mind and wants to leave, you will have to consider the options. Seek advice from your accountant.

• The partnership will generally benefit from all your income, wherever/however generated – unless specifically excluded (with (all) your partner(s)'s agreement).

6.2(c) Limited company

The limited company has a distinct legal, financial, and commercial identity separate from those of its owners/managers. It is somewhat more complex and more expensive to run, as you have the following extra costs:

• NI contributions are at a higher level than for the sole trader or partnership as you will be deemed to be an employee and the company will pay the employer's NI contributions on any salary you take in addition to you paying your own NI under PAYE.

• Accounts and audit are more formal and vary according to the size of the company. There is now no audit requirement for the smallest companies but it may be a condition of bank borrowing that an audit is carried out – or you may wish to have an accountant's review for your own satisfaction.

• Company filing fees, formation and legal fees etc.

• More information has to be kept and also filed with the authorities.

There are a number of types of companies, but for most purposes there are three main types that will be of interest:

1 A quoted public company (plc).
2 A public company (plc).
3 A private company (Ltd).

A quoted or listed company is a plc which has met the stringent reporting and other requirements of a recognised Stock Exchange and which may accordingly be able to invite public subscription for its shares (subject to meeting all the legal formalities). It will not be an appropriate vehicle for most readers, but if you are considering operating through a quoted plc, you will certainly need professional advice. A public company (plc) which is unquoted – again unlikely to involve most readers – has less stringent legal requirements imposed on it than a quoted plc, but more requirements than a private company, including having an authorised, issued and paid-up share capital of at least £50,000.

A private company (or 'Ltd') is described in the Companies Act as a company 'which is not a public company'. It must have one director and a different person as company secretary, and a minimum paid-up share capital of £1 (out of, say, £100 authorised share capital). It can either be formed for you/by you or you can buy one 'off the shelf' (from a specialist or from a lawyer/ accountant/ company secretary) which, together with any necessary change of name, will probably cost about £300 or so. Legislation places a number of requirements on private companies, including the need to prepare company accounts, to have them audited (dependent on size), to complete annual returns, to file accounts with Companies House, and to display the company name together with other required details* on all key stationery and on the premises appropriately. (*Includes company name, Registered Company Number, trading office, registered office, where registered, i.e. Registered in England/ England and Wales/ Wales/ Scotland/ Ireland, details of all directors or no directors (but NB foreign directors), VAT number on invoices (if registered for VAT). Discuss with your lawyer.) There are also rules governing the obligations and responsibilities of directors.

Limited companies have the benefit of **limiting the shareholders' liabilities,** i.e. if the business fails, the creditors cannot (in most circumstances) sue the directors/shareholders personally, in the absence of fault on their part. However, as founders/directors, you may be required (by banks for example) to pledge your personal assets to guarantee the debts of the company – which may rather negate the benefits of limited liability. Furthermore, the courts (and Revenue and Customs) have started to look behind the limited company 'veil' and there can be circumstances where the limited company protections are not applicable, and the directors can be personally liable.

All companies can continue in their separate existence without the founding directors and/or shareholders, and after sale by, or the death of, a founder. If you are going into business with others in a company, you should **prepare a shareholders' agreement** (almost certainly with advice from your lawyer) setting out the business objectives including growth and long term ownership plans, who invests what/how, shareholdings, shares of profits, entitlement to dividends/salaries, who does what, the effect of different hours, holidays, retirement, closure, sale, how shareholders/executives leave etc (as for partnerships) and what happens to their shares (do they have to sell them and at what price, or can they keep them).

Other issues include that it may be **easier to raise finance**, or to sell the business at a later date, for a limited company than for other forms of business. There are also strict controls on the naming of companies, which you can explore with your lawyer/accountant. This latter control can give you a business protection – if your business name is valuable to your marketing, it would be possible, for example, to register a company, but to trade as a sole trader.

6.2 (d)   Limited liability partnership

It is now possible to set up a limited liability partnership (LLP). This is another form of company with its own separate identity. It has many of the characteristics of the limited company, but some of the flexibility of a partnership, including taxation treatment. As a relatively new form of business structure, case law is still developing and you should certainly seek advice if you think this structure may be appropriate. The registration formalities of a limited partnership **must** be complied with.

It is essential that you take advice before committing yourself to one form of business absolutely; it is possible to change from one to another, but there is a cost involved. If in doubt, it is probably reasonable to start your business as a sole trader while you consider the full implications.

6.3 Some other issues to be addressed

6.3(a) The market image of the business

Possibly the most important 'other issue' is the **market perception** of your business. In order to be credible and credit-worthy in the marketplace, you may be better to trade as a limited company and the very fact that you are able to put 'Ltd' or 'Limited' after your business name may allow you (for example) to buy goods on credit, get trade discounts, or to convince your customers that your business is larger than it might appear if you were trading as an individual. Corporate status seems to be perceived as higher than for sole traders and can lead to corporate credit rating by independent agencies, and, for example, banks may find it easier to take a floating charge on company assets to secure their loan than to look at private assets. You may also find that some organisations will be reluctant to trade with a business that is not a limited company.

6.3(b) In business on your own or with others?

If it is possible that you will need the help of others with some of the projects or business that you undertake, the form of a limited company may enable you to present a more united image to your customers. This does not necessarily mean that the other people need to be shareholders/directors in your company, nor necessarily employees. It is possible for a sole trader, or a partnership, or a limited company to engage others (whether they are sole traders, partnerships or limited companies), but it is perhaps less easy to sell the concept of a united front in marketing terms to your customer unless you are all 'part of the same organisation'. This is most easily effected as a company.

6.3(c) Complexity

Setting up as a sole trader is a relatively simple process and the formation documentation, the records and accounts that must be kept, and the filing of information with the 'authorities' are all much simpler.

Overall the sole trader route is likely to be the least costly route of all four – the external services required for preparing accounts, auditing accounts, corporation tax advice and Company Secretarial duties for a company could easily cost you in excess of £1,000 per annum, but perhaps less than one half of this being a sole trader (note there is no requirement on a sole trader to have accounts or audits, or indeed an external accountant, although records must be kept, but it may be to your advantage in dealing with the bank or tax authorities or others).

The company's annual return and the company accounts, both of which must be filed publicly, also give rise to financial and other information being published about the company's trading, as well as information on the directors and the shareholders that would not be the case as a sole trader.

6.3(d) National Insurance

National Insurance is radically different between the status of sole trader or partner and that of a company. As a sole trader/partner, your liability to NI comes under Class 2 and Class 4 contributions, calculation of the latter being based on taxable profits less allowable deductions. The benefit of this is that the NI contributions are lower than for companies, but because these contributions are much lower than as an employed person, your entitlement to state benefits will be reduced as a result.

Operating through a limited company, you will be a director and/or employee of the company and your company will be paying you (almost certainly) under the PAYE system, with contributions to NI being paid both by you and by your employer (your company) both being at a much higher rate than if you were a sole trader. The calculations are more complex too. You are not obliged to pay yourself entirely by salary – some payment can be made as dividends which currently do not attract NI, but can result in other potential benefits being lost (e.g. on Corporation Tax). Revenue and Customs have been addressing this area particularly in recent years, so discuss this with your accountant. (Check Chapter 12 for special tax rules regarding consultants and freelancers.)

6.3(e) Tax

There are four aspects to tax with regard to 'own-business' namely:

1   the expenses you can deduct from your income before tax is levied
2   the rate of tax you pay
3   when you pay the tax
4   the offsetting of losses against tax.

As a sole trader, any deductible costs are set against your income as a sole trader. As a company, some expenses and costs are set against company income, others against your salary. There are differences under tax legislation as to how business profits are calculated but these are not significant and should certainly not be the sole reason for choosing one form of operation over another.

As a sole trader, the rate of tax on any profit you make will be at the normal income tax rates after your personal allowances. In a limited company, corporation tax is charged on profits you leave in the business (i.e. profit after all business costs and after deducting your salary) which will (initially, at least!) be at the small company rate. The money you pay yourself by way of a salary (which is a cost for the company) will be paid to you net of NI and normal income tax after your personal allowances (as it would for any employee). Any profits after tax you take out of the company as dividends may (if appropriate) be subject to additional income tax later at your top marginal rate, but currently these dividends will not be liable to personal or company NI contributions. (But see Chapter 12, as in 6.3(d) above).

There are some special rules governing the start-up and close down phases of a sole trader or partnership but when operational, you would normally pay tax on a current year basis – by paying instalments in advance of filing your tax return. Within a limited company, you must pay over the PAYE tax deducted from employees each month to Revenue and Customs, and Corporation Tax on company profits is normally paid over nine months after the end of the accounting year. Special rules apply for new companies. Delayed payment of the full tax due under sole trader/partnership rules can provide (cheap) much-needed working capital, the adverse effect of this delay is that cash must be available to pay the tax immediately when due so as not to incur stiff penalties.

If you think it likely that you will make losses initially in your new business, the rules regarding carry forward/carry back and offsetting against other income are more generous as a sole trader/partnership than as a limited company. However, companies can generally set trading losses against chargeable capital gains in the same year. Seek your accountant's advice!

It is worth noting that if you are operating as a limited company, any corporate liabilities for VAT, and for Income Tax and NI under PAYE, may result in personal liability for the directors if the company funds are diverted, or if payments to Revenue and Customs are not made; the courts may take a tougher line on Government debts than on other creditors.

6.3(f) Pension requirements

Personal pension requirements is another area where professional advice is strongly recommended. As a generality, the ability of a limited company to invest in a pension scheme is substantially higher than for an individual, but it is important to review your plans in the light of already accrued benefits and the current legislation as contributions and/or benefits may be limited where substantial benefits already exist. Pension advisors must be authorised to offer such advice and a good one is usually well worth engaging as this is a very complex area. (NB – major changes in pensions legislation are planned for April 2006.)

6.3(g) Longer term plans for the business

If you need to raise money from financial institutions, the stock market, or from venture capital organisations to establish/expand your business or to acquire another, or alternatively, are envisaging building up a major business that you will want to sell on at some stage, then it is likely that the limited company route will be most attractive.

You may wish to involve others in the business, in a 'sleeping' capacity, i.e. with limited risk/exposure, such as friends/relatives to help with funding or minors/trustees of family settlements as a way of distributing family wealth. In this case, a limited company would be the most attractive vehicle.

6.3(h) VAT

In general, the decision on whether or not to register for VAT will be taken independently from choosing the format for operating. However, if your customers are primarily VAT registered businesses themselves, it is probably preferable for you to register for VAT whether or not you are required by law to do so. This is because the requirement to register is related to annual turnover and any business not registered for VAT is either very small or very new. Is this the impression you wish to leave with your clients? However, if your customers are mainly private, non-VAT-registered individuals, or if they are businesses whose supplies are wholly or partially exempt from

VAT, then registration for VAT will materially increase your prices to them.

Specific detailed advice on VAT registration is obtainable from your local Revenue and Customs office in a leaflet *'Should I be registered for VAT?'*. The administration procedures for VAT are not complex for someone running a business sensibly and professionally, with adequate records, but you must remember to 'put aside' the VAT you owe, as it must be paid on time or penalties will be applied.

6.3(i) Other legal issues

You may need to meet other legal requirements to run your business and it will be your responsibility to establish what you have to do to meet these. ('Ignorance of the law is no excuse'). Other 'legals' include:

- Getting a license to operate your business (e.g. a nursing home)
- Planning permission
- Legally required insurance (employer's insurance) – as well as commercially desirable insurances such as public liability, goods, cash etc
- Health and safety legislation
- Environmental requirements and legislation
- Employment law (including minimum wages, flexible working, equal opportunities)
- Data protection – if storing anyone's personal details
- Product/service/commercial liability protection
- Industry specific legislation, e.g. in Financial Services
- Other general legislation affecting all businesses such as the Disability Discrimination Act (regarding access to goods and services).

6.4 Advice sources

Contact your local Revenue and Customs offices, and other Government offices for their range of advisory leaflets. You are likely to find that government offices have become much more approachable for 'first-timers' with a range of introductory materials including videos and training courses.

If you do not have a lawyer, contact:

> Lawyers for Your Business
> The Law Society, 113 Chancery Lane, London, WC2A 1PL
> Telephone: 020 7405 9075
> **www.lawsoc.org.uk**

They can provide a list of solicitors in your area who will, as part of the 'Lawyers for Your Business Scheme', provide a free-of-charge initial consultation to discuss your plans.

To find suitable accountants, you can contact:

> The Association of Corporate & Certified Accountants
> 64 Finnieston Street, Glasgow G3 8DT
> Tel: 0141 582 2000
> **www.acca.co.uk/finding_an_accountant**

> The Chartered Institute of Management Accountants
> 26 Chapter Street, London SW1P 4NP
> Tel: 020 7663 5441
> **www.cimaglobal.com/main/resources/services**

> The Institute of Chartered Accountants in Scotland
> CA House, 21 Haymarket Yards,
> Edinburgh EH12 5BH
> Tel: 0131 3470100
> **www.icas.org.uk**

> The Institute of Chartered Accountants of England & Wales
> PO Box 433, Moorgate Place, London EC2P 2BJ
> Telephone: 020 7628 7060
> **www.icaewfirms.co.uk/database/locsearch.asp**

They can provide the address/phone of the local branch, which can then put you in touch with local practising accountants. The best course is to have someone recommended to you!

The Government publishes a wide range of information (including the No-Nonsense Guide to Government rules and regulations for setting up your business – from Business Link or **www.dti.gov.uk/publications**.

See also Appendix V – Useful addresses

And don't forget the internet and search engines such as **www.google.com**

See also Appendix 1 – Further Reading

Two very useful books from Management Books 2000 Ltd

Taxation Simplified, edited by James Alexander and published annually just after the (usually) March Budget

The Private Company Secretary's Handbook, edited by James Alexander and Michael Harris, new edition published in February 2006

6.5   Key points

- **In considering your choice of business identity, factor in your own personal objectives and whether you give priority to (for example) marketing issues rather than tax, or financial issues rather than marketing etc. Complete a check list approach on all the issues covered above.**

- **Your reasons for choosing one legal form over another may be for image or marketing purposes, but remember the tax and NI effects.**

- **Changing your mind later is possible, but may be expensive.**

- **Get good advice.**

- **Complete a checklist of all the above points to help you decide on the form your business should take.**

- .

- .

- .

7

Tax, VAT, National Insurance and Administration

7.1   Introduction

'In this world nothing is certain except death and taxes,' said Benjamin Franklin and it's certainly true that in starting your own business, you will learn lots more about all sorts of taxes. Governments keep promising to make life easier for smaller business, but still the legislators manage to keep the small businessman tearing his hair out. Forms to fill in, taxes to pay – the only consolation being 'If the Government is getting so much, then I must be getting something'! This chapter highlights some of the key tax issues (NI being a form of tax) and leads you to ask the more detailed questions of your accountant or tax advisor – or even the revenue collector's website.

This chapter then looks at some of the other administrative issues for the smaller businessman.

7.2   Taxation, including VAT

7.2(a)   V A T

VAT is a tax on sales which you will pay on most of your purchases and, if you are registered for VAT, which you will charge all your customers. Although called a tax, VAT is actually classified as a 'duty' and is collected separately from income and corporation taxes. You must register for VAT if your turnover exceeds or is likely to exceed a given amount, which is normally set annually in the Budget (£60,000 from 1 April 2005). Registration may be advantageous to you even if you are not required to so do, as you will then be able to recover the VAT you have paid to your suppliers by charging VAT to your customers, and also confirming the impression you wish to give clients and suppliers about your business. The difference between the VAT you collect and what you pay is either paid to, or recovered from Revenue and Customs probably on a monthly or quarterly basis.

To register should present no worries, especially as better provisions now exist under the 'Cash Accounting' scheme to safeguard you from losing the VAT on a sale that later becomes a bad debt. This scheme is one of several schemes (cash accounting, flat percentage, annual schemes) aimed at the smaller business and may be elected where turnover is below a limit (normally revised annually).

You should check with the local Revenue and Customs (VAT) office as early as possible to ask whether and to what extent the tax applies to your particular business and on their other requirements regarding invoices, receipts, books and records.

7.2(b) Income tax

You will already know that in paid employment your earnings are taxed under PAYE for the tax year ended on 5th April. This status of paid employment generally includes the situation where you solely own the company that is paying you. When running a business as a sole trader or partnership, you are instead taxed on your net profit, adjusted by Revenue and Custom's rules for depreciation and any other relevant items. You may choose any date as the year-end for your annual accounts and the choice can make a cash flow difference, so take professional advice as the choice can delay significant sums of tax. The actual tax is normally payable in two instalments on 31 January and 31 July. The January instalment will normally be accompanied by a balancing payment or claim for repayment for the previous tax year.

You can charge a variety of items against profits, some of which may need negotiating with the Inspector of Taxes. It is usually best to leave this to your accountant, who will also cover the following important areas:

- advising on the date to end your financial year
- explaining any special rules for the start-up and cessation of business
- telling you what you can charge against income, especially for the use of your private house, but so as to avoid any risk of a Capital Gains assessment on it, or any part of it
- providing details of the tax reliefs available when you retire and sell your business.

7.2(c)   Corporation Tax

This tax is paid by companies on their adjusted net profit and the tax rates are lower for companies with small profits. Tax is normally payable nine months after the end of the accounting period.

To minimise your tax, you should discuss your company's likely results with your accountant at least one month before the year end. The results may be amended retrospectively by way of your own director's remuneration for that year, how much you wish to leave as company profit, and how much you wish to take as dividend. The procedure is perfectly legal and ethical, and enables you to balance your own income tax and the company's corporation tax liability as suits you best.

7.3   National Insurance and pensions

7.3(a)   National Insurance

On the assumption that you have left your previous job, you should register with the Government offices as 'Unemployed' as soon as possible. This will ensure that your NI contributions are credited from the appropriate date until your new venture is deemed to start trading, thus continuing your entitlement to any employment/unemployment benefits and maintaining your contributions to state pension. You are unlikely to be able to draw unemployment benefit initially because of the technicalities of the notice period – the rules are tightly drawn.

There are a number of types of NI contributions, three of which are of most relevance to most 'own-business' people:

- Class 1 for employed persons.
- Class 2 and Class 4 for self-employed persons.

You are deemed to be self-employed if you are a sole trader or a partner in a firm. You are an employed person if you are working for someone else, irrespective of whether that person is a sole trader, partnership or limited company. It is important to calculate the effect on your contributions – for example, a husband and wife running a limited company and drawing equal remuneration will pay substantially more in NI than a sole trader who takes all the profits and whose spouse is paid just the amount of the 'Lower Earnings Limit'. This is largely because a company situation calls for contributions from both the employer (i.e. the company) and the employee. Reductions in NI contributions should not be the main reason for choosing self-employment as a sole trader!

As an employer, under legislation covering NI, Income Tax, and Corporation Tax, you are legally obliged to supply the authorities with various documents annually to show details of tax and NI which has been deducted and paid over. Currently, these are supplied as 'hard copy' but substantial progress is being made towards electronic filing of such information which will soon become a requirement. Visit **www.direct.gov.uk** or **www.gateway.gov.uk** for more information and guidance.

7.3(b) Pensions

The provision of pensions advice is controlled by legislation and advisors must be suitable qualified and registered. I cannot seek to advise you at all on this complex area but it has been reliably estimated that it costs about 20% of annual salary between the ages of 25 and 65 to provide a pension of two-thirds of final salary. If you also want to provide some inflation proofing, perhaps a widow's pension, life cover, and 'death in service' benefits for dependents, the costs can increase dramatically – to say 30% of salary. Any delay in starting contributions increases the needed contributions – a five year delay could mean the need to double annual contributions to achieve the same pension fund level.

This gives you an idea of the overall funding costs. It is therefore most important to set up a well funded personal pension plan and take advantage of the tax legislation that provides tax relief on contributions. (NB a major overhaul of the tax regime for pensions is due to take effect in April 2006.) Your pension scheme contributions are normally allowable against taxable income within certain limits and can be especially advantageous for higher rate taxpayers.

A company earning substantial profits can generally make larger contributions than an individual into pension schemes.

This area is becoming more complex as a result of legislation, despite promises to simplify matters. Specialist advice is strongly recommended, especially if you already have substantial pension benefits or accrued entitlements from a former employer, or if you need to offer access to stakeholder pensions or set up an employer's pension scheme for your employees (if you have five or more). Some sensible guidance can be found in *Pensions Simplified* by Tony Granger, published by MB2000.

7.4   Premises and equipment

If you are going to **work from home**, you will want to ensure that such use is both legal and tax-effective. Your accountant can probably advise, in your particular circumstances, on making best use of the available reliefs. You should establish whether running your proposed business from home is affected by planning restrictions, any restrictions in the lease or freehold deeds, and whether any permission from local authorities, building societies etc. are necessary. It is possible that, by running a business from your home, you may move (part of) your house into the orbit of business rates. You will also need to consider the effect on existing, and the need for new, insurances. Establish how the business may affect the capital gains tax exemption on (all or part of) your private house.

Whilst on the subject of working from home, if this is a possibility for you, consider in some detail how it will work for you and your family. For some, it is ideal to 'commute' to work in seconds, while others find it impossible to settle down to work at home. Another see-saw is the pressure that home life can have on work (interrupting work with those left-over jobs or pleasurable tasks/events) or vice-versa at weekends or evenings. (One of my clients spoke of his 'briefcase looking at him coldly on Saturday mornings' when he was home-based.) If you are working from home, you will need a practical, effective system for managing your working time.

With some businesses, **separate premises** are immediately required, e.g. for setting up a retail shop (see Chapter 13). Apart from the costs of acquiring the premises, a number of other issues need consideration including the ability to attract passing trade from people walking by – cheap premises on the edge of town may prove more expensive than a town centre property with high 'footfall'. What image do you wish to create with your customers? What about attracting staff and the impression you give to suppliers? Issues such as Health and Safety legislation may affect you if, for example, you are opening a food shop/stall.

Should you decide to acquire separate business premises, you may find that you need to write your Business Plan before you have settled the details of these premises and related costs. If so, budget generously for the initial settling-in costs and for ongoing expenses. Prepare a sketch of your requirements and work out the costs based on square footage. A wise approach should broadly follow these lines.

- Decide upon the locality: consider the feasibility and possible benefits of any areas of the country entitled to Government subsidies.

- Seek a locality where business prospects look likely to improve rather than decline. Check for anything like new motorways, bypasses, railways and property developments that could affect your business.

- Find out about security and restrictive covenants for usage, planning and fire regulations (obtain a copy of the existing certificate) and dilapidation penalties at the end of the lease. Can you gain easy and legal access to the building at all times?

- Obtain advice from your solicitor about the details of your particular deed or lease, license or purchase agreement, including the termination clauses.

- Have a full survey carried out by professional surveyors of all properties, whether rented/leased or purchased.

- If possible, obtain estimates for making repairs, alterations or extensions and for all equipment. Establish who pays (usually you!) for any work on the property and when you need landlord's permission.

- As soon as practicable, rework your estimates of cost to include actual figures for rent, rates, power/light/heat, phones etc.

- Remember that a lease is a major expense item – it is difficult to escape the terms of a lease (even if you get someone else to 'stand in your shoes' for the rent). It is a commitment possibly for many years.

- What about expansion of the business in due course? Will you need to move in one year's time or five year's time?

- Consult your accountant on the tax implications of acquiring a freehold or leasehold. It is important to appreciate that many of the outlays may be non-allowable for tax. Alterations and equipment may rank for capital allowances over a period of years: some items, probably smaller, can be charged in the current year as revenue expenditure.

7.5 Staff

The costs of employing someone are probably about twice their salary – if you take into account National Insurance, pension contributions, holidays and sickness, office space and equipment, other expenses, company car and (possibly) profit-share. Employing staff also opens up new areas to consider – meeting the career and other aspirations and needs of your staff and the **legal requirements** of an employer – for example, a contract/terms and conditions of employment must be given after an initial statutory period to any employee, including most part-timers, and laws and regulations covering non-discrimination, statutory requirements on working time and holidays etc, health and safety, and the requirement for a number of other records to be kept. This all calls for a substantial investment of your time.

Having put the disadvantages and difficulties first, if you are to grow your 'own-business' it is almost certain that at some stage you will want or need to expand your team; it is now up to you to make a case for taking on people, at any level, and to provide for all their employment needs. Who will you need? What qualities, skills, personality, etc? Can you train, offer long term careers? What are the costs? What about holiday and sick cover? How will you recruit and when?

Salaried employees need not be the only solution. Apart from agencies to cover a temporary need, you could also use consultants, freelancers, specialists and piece-workers for many kinds of work. Probably the most important point for a small business is that there is little room for lame ducks and you will need to be as certain as possible of the success of a permanent appointment before entering into such a commitment. Official guidance on employment matters can be obtained from Revenue and Customs, the Department of Social Security, your lawyer, and from ACAS, as well as (for example) the Chartered Institute of Personnel and Development (CIPD).

A word of warning – whatever you do, don't be tempted to offer 'cash in hand' to your staff to 'save tax', 'avoid paperwork' or 'save on VAT'. There are severe penalties for tax evasion.

7.6 Training and advice

There are two schools of thought to be explored under this heading.

The first argues that if you feel you are the right kind of person and have found a commercial opportunity, then you should press ahead as quickly as is reasonably possible and allow the rest of the learning curve to take place on the job.

The alternate view is that a tailor-made course could prove worthwhile, especially for those with little administrative experience. This could specifically cover business plan preparation, marketing and selling, accounting, taxation, and some law, and would take place in a group environment to ensure that participants could draw from one another over the period of some days. There are many courses available giving training in becoming self-employed, which run from 1 – 5 days, costing from £250 to £500 per day.

Training provided by the Local Education Authority and Adult Education Centres will almost certainly be provided to the unemployed at reduced rates. Free training which is sometimes provided in business planning and for new business ventures by Government organisations is often well worth-while and this can also include a wide range of other advice and training. Schemes may vary from area to area. Contact the local office of the Department of Industry for more information. Other sources of advice can include the Chamber of Commerce, trade associations, commercial training organisations – or any other entrepreneur!

7.7 Professional advisors

It is most important to have **good professional advisors** who can be called upon as needs arise. These advisors should also be appropriate to businesses of the size you are starting and may well not be the most familiar names in their profession. The best way to be assured of their suitability is to have them recommended by friends or colleagues as being relevant, suitable, and good – this is absolutely NOT a 'Yellow Pages' exercise. However, if you are likely to require specialist advice, e.g. to negotiate a technical trade agreement involving a European or international partner, then you might be wise to use an apparently expensive legal firm that has the relevant experience and expertise, rather than pay a smaller practitioner to learn with you.

In choosing and using a specialist advisor, **be clear what services you require** and prepare a written specification, ask others for recommendations and meet a shortlist of people within each firm who will be providing the advice – not just the marketing partner! Remember, their time is charged for, often on an hourly basis and at different rates for partners, managers and staff, and may also vary according to the perceived risks of the transaction.

The particular advisors who should be in place by the time of starting up are:

Bankers. Do not be afraid to hold discussions with more than one. Ask carefully about costs, interest rates and annual 'Facility' fees and get it in writing. There is no such thing as a friendly loan and bankers have been known to warm up customers with one rate of interest, only to find a reason later on for charging another higher rate.

Accountants. You should **ask for advice at the outset** about the format of the business, keeping the records required by law, records needed to operate and manage the business, tax implications and the annual accounts and audit. This will enable you to ensure your books meet legal needs and to minimise the professional costs at the year-end. Whilst you must **meet the legal requirements** regarding records and accounts etc, in my view, the key requirements is to ensure that your books give you sufficient information to run your business effectively and it may pay you to talk to other similarly employed people about business management information requirements (accountants do prefer to see 'proper books'!)

Insurance and pension brokers. Apart from making sure that your **legal obligations** regarding insurance are covered, you should also consider sensible commercial risk cover for the business, insurance against loss or damage for the physical items you use in the business, and policies for any other relevant items. The total list is too long for this book but includes, for example, life insurance (to replace that provided by a former employer?), employer's liability, consequential loss or damage, loss of profit and other business risks, professional indemnity, keyman, medical expenses, long-term sickness and accident insurance. In the area of life assurance and pensions, there may be relevant tax concessions that encourage starting a scheme without delay.

Legal, trade marks and patent agents. Whilst there are specialist advisors in each of these areas and such advice at an early stage can be invaluable, your solicitor should either be able to guide you through the early stages or refer you to the appropriate specialist.

Estate or property agents. The use of specialist advice may not be relevant to your business, but it could be wise to have your house valued to establish your private net asset position in case you need this for securing bank borrowings. A mortgage on good residential property is usually the cheapest way of borrowing. You may be able to structure a loan for business purposes secured on your house but your primary lender will have to consent to the additional security being given.

Check with all your advisors whether you require any special permission, licences, approvals, formal training, association memberships, insurances etc to be allowed to operate your business.

7.8 Setting up your IT system

This may sound a grand heading when you are only considering perhaps using your home computer for records, but the use of IT (including the internet) has become an essential part of most business operations. Even the Government is encouraging use of IT, both in the form of tax concessions for its acquisition and in supplying/requesting information through the use of IT. The use of the internet is referred to elsewhere, so this section focuses on the basic IT system issues.

In the context of your 'own-business', IT covers phone, mobile, fax, PC (possibly networked?), printer, internet access, point-of-sale equipment including tills, together with all related software and security (access, data protection, and virus protection). Overall, this is likely to be one of your major start-up costs.

Try to specify your needs under each of the above categories. What do you need to start in business and how might you need to expand in the first year or two?

For contact with customers, most businesses (even individuals operating part-time from home) will have a business phone (and possibly a fax as well), mobile, and a business or acceptable private email address. Consider using broadband services if appropriate.

For your PC system, consider your overall needs. If you are going to spend a lot of time 'on the road' perhaps a laptop (although materially more expensive than a desktop) would be the answer. If you need more than one PC for staff, at what point does a network become viable – to share data, to access each other's information and so on? You will probably need to be using four or more PCs regularly for a network to be needed, but check this with advisors.

On the software front, word-processing and spreadsheets are more or less essential for office based businesses (I'll refer to accounting software in Chapter 16 'Simple records, accounts and book-keeping'). If you need (as most of us do!) to keep customer details easily accessible, contact management or PIM software can be a real boon. Similarly, businesses selling people skills by the hour may benefit from software allowing job-costing and time-booking.

Whilst email may be one of your preferred communication media, think too about the benefits or otherwise of maintaining your own website to solicit contact (as well as for marketing).

Two areas often neglected until problems arise are getting independent professional advice on the IT equipment and software needed and getting technical and service support lined up before it is needed to solve business-critical problems. See if you can get referrals from contacts on both areas.

Plan too for your training needs – better to think about it before you start rather than when you are in the thick of dealing with customers and need to take a couple of days off for that essential PC training.

7.9 Key points

- **If your turnover is below the level where you are legally obliged to register for VAT, it may still be worth registering (if you are in business-to-business selling).**

- **Taxes are inevitable, as is form-filling to meet statutory requirements.**

- **Get your administration ideas sorted out before you start.**

- **At long last you are in charge of all the details. So don't complain!**

- **Especially in your new areas of responsibility, don't be afraid to ask for advice.**

- **If employing staff, don't be tempted to offer 'cash in hand' and avoid paperwork.**

- .

- .

- .

8

Some Business Options

8.1 Introduction

Whilst there is a huge range of types of businesses you could consider, and a number of ways in which you can get into your 'own-business', perhaps some of the most common may be grouped as follows:

- Retailing goods and/or services
- Consultancy and freelancing
- Trading and manufacturing
- Business services
- Portfolio, part-time, and pre-retirement
- Franchising*
- Buying a business*

*The last two are forms of 'buying into a business'

Some of the key issues involved in each of the above are dealt with in this chapter. Whatever your venture, a common thread for you will be the need to develop a Business Plan, both for your own use and for that of anyone else interested in the venture – bankers, family, accountant and so on. This is dealt with in more detail later.

8.2 Retailing goods and/or services

Some see the retail sector as the backbone of the commercial world. Certainly many will see the opening of a shop, or a restaurant, or possibly the supply of plumbing, garage, or market research services as the only way they want to start in business. Face-to-face with your customers every day – some see it as a delight, others as a challenge. Whichever of these appeals to you, there is a myriad of small shops and businesses providing all manner of goods and services, with new faces coming into the market every day.

There are relatively easy ways to enter the retail market which do not require significant entry costs, e.g. as a jobbing carpenter or part-time market researcher. It doesn't always follow that where the entry is easy and entry costs low, success is guaranteed or that losses will be minimal – losses have a way of creeping up on you! One thing no-one is short of in the retail sector is the opportunity to do market research – we are all consumers. Other issues may be more difficult than you thought, e.g. costs might be higher, the whole area of property, legislative/planning controls, other market forces. Research carefully before you jump. It could make all the difference.

Certain parts of the market are very **stringently controlled** by legislation – food, for example – and if you have no prior experience, significant research in this area will be essential. Similarly, knowledge of the range of suppliers, standard mark-ups, ways of marketing which work and so on all come from prior knowledge and save you time and cost. Possibly the best way of learning is at someone else's cost – work in the industry before you start out on your own.

One required facility in this market which could cause you a delay in starting up is arranging the facility for credit card payments. This can take your bank several weeks to arrange, even if you have been a regular and long-standing customer. If you believe it is essential for your business, you will need to plan ahead!

Probably the most important issue for shop premises will be shop location. The other key issue will be your attitude to customers and service – which is where the smaller retailer can win hands-down against the chain stores. Exceptional service could make all the difference.

Special issues for the retail market are considered in Chapter 13.

8.3 Consultancy and freelancing

Working as a consultant or freelance may have a number of attractions as a way of starting your 'own-business'. If this is to be your main source of income, you must be sure that, as an alternative to employment, this route will provide an adequate income plus pension provision, over many years. As a 'top-up' to already secured income, the choice may be easier. In either case, the Business Plan can be a comparatively simple document by comparison with, say, a trading venture, but it must nevertheless be fairly specific about your marketing methods, clientele, charge-out rates and expected results.

You may be able to start by using your core skills with previous employers and their associates, suppliers and customers. This has the added advantage that you are likely to be operating in a market sector with which you are familiar and with people you may know. For long term security of income, you will almost certainly need to build on this within a fairly short time to establish a sufficient customer base.

In putting your plan into operation, your time will be divided between marketing/sales, administration, and chargeable hours. If you were employed by a professional firm, you would be required to keep a daily log sheet to account for your time. Although this may at first seem an unnecessary chore for a sole practitioner, it is a wise discipline to follow. When totalled for each working week, it will soon show a trend of how the time has been spent proportionately among the three activities mentioned above. This in turn will give vital management information about whether the overall plan is really on track.

You should, of course, have the usual professional advisors and go through all the procedures mentioned earlier, but the path to success in this type of business more than any other is in your commitment to success and the effective use of your own working hours. It is definitely **not the easy option** many believe it to be.

If you build an established practice and engage staff or partners, you may create a saleable asset for when you retire. This will bring a bonus, possibly substantial, to your income and should be borne in mind when considering whether to retire or continue at a lower level of activity.

Special issues for consultants are considered further in Chapter 12.

8.4 Trading and manufacturing

If you plan to start a business in either of these areas, you are likely to need rather more experience in the business operations than for running a consultancy, especially regarding the marketing and sales side. There is inherently **more risk** in trading and manufacturing and quite possibly an **opportunity for greater reward** too.

The risk factor is very real and should be emphasised. Traders run the risk of buying stock which does not shift and manufacturers can incur substantial losses if, after buying plant and materials, and then paying labour and other overheads in manufacturing the product, they cannot sell their products. You must therefore know your market and your margins thoroughly in order to keep your business on an even keel.

You must also be prepared to cope with far more regulations, i.e. those that cover factories, shops and offices, as well as further specialist rules that relate to specific trades. Your business plan must cover all these items as well as the usual things – it is important that no hidden or forgotten costs emerge once the business has been launched.

Manufacturing is possibly the **most complex** of business areas, involving more operational stages in bringing together the components needed to make, package and dispatch the finished product. Except where selling into an existing competitive market, the ultimate price to the customer is likely to be broadly determined by the manufacturer, as the profit margins for wholesaling and retailing will probably have been well established by existing practice. Price will particularly need to take notice of competition.

Wholesaling principally depends on being able to buy well and to turn over sufficient quantities of goods at established profit margins to cover the overhead costs. Only practical experience will show how successful this can be; the risk of a down-turn in volumes, especially in wholesaling, is always the factor to be watched most closely. Unless it is caused by a general slowing of the economy, trading in a wider range of products may provide some safeguard. Some industries will be more susceptible to fashion, leading to much earlier potential stock loss. Many of the issues raised in Chapter 13 for retailing will be relevant to traders/wholesalers.

8.5 Business services

A different form of business-to-business enterprise is the provision of business services. This is in many ways akin to providing consultancy services – from a marketing point of view – but involves the employment of others. This could be the provision of a range of personnel supplying consultancy services, contract or specialist cleaning, secretarial or professional services, maintenance services etc.

Risks will be greater than for the sole practitioner, due to the costs of employing staff (whether or not they are 'booked out') and the possibly higher premises and equipment needs. This can be offset by the potential for major gain – if the 'sums' are right, due to the profit margins on staff/services supplied. Review other operations in the marketplace and the providers of other services as part of your business planning exercise.

A more detailed review is provided in Chapter 14.

8.6 Portfolio, part-time, and pre-retirement roles

Many people do not want or need to seek a full-time role to provide all their income and pension requirements. For various reasons they may seek to supplement a pension or other income, from one or more part-time roles, roles undertaken not wholly for financial reasons – or not for any financial reason, or a mixture of such roles (or a 'portfolio' approach).

All of the criteria set out earlier will still apply, but may need to be 'tuned' for your own criteria for success in this category. It may be, for example, that you 'want to put something back into society' and see yourself undertaking voluntary, charity or pro-bono work for little or no financial benefit. Your criteria would then include working for something which really inspires you. It would be a mistake to assume that charities necessarily want your skills. The charity market is competitive in its own right and just wanting to help will not be enough. It is very likely, unless you are working through your personal network, that you will still be seeking such a job against heavy competition.

Or perhaps you are seeking to start out on a part-time basis because of other commitments (e.g. family or hobbies) and can only invest part of your working week in the job – or maybe you want to wind down towards retirement. In either event, understand the implications of this in relation to the organisation that you will work for, and in career terms for you.

Another area for consideration for senior managers relates to non-executive directorships (NEDs). To attract such directorships, you are likely to be well connected in your field of expertise and held in high regard. Offers of such posts may well come your way without you actively seeking them, but they are unlikely to be easy to find. There are organisations that specialise or undertake recruitment for NEDs and you should approach these as professionally as if you were job-seeking. A few reminders about such appointments:

- NEDs must be independent, and able to probe and assess other board members. The role is temporary (say up to three years) and many NEDs are not well paid.
- They will always be short of information.
- They have the same legal liabilities as other directors but have less time and information; take out insurance if appropriate.
- Demand for such positions very substantially outweighs the number available.

Another alternative is part-time or short-term consultancy projects – comments elsewhere in this book on consultancy generally apply, except that a lower level of commitment may be required in due course, once the business is established.

An excellent book about the portfolio life is *You ... Unlimited* by Colin McCrudden et al, published by MB2000.

8.7 Franchising

Much of this book is written for people who are starting their 'own-business' from scratch. Another approach to running your 'own-business' is franchising, although this clearly **offers less autonomy**. Franchising involves paying an up-front fee and a regular monthly percentage of sales in exchange for being provided with a **proven business model**, plus training and support, often with the benefit of corporate advertising – to which you contribute. You may also benefit from a well-known trading name. It is often thought of as being related mainly to retail businesses, but there are other types of business e.g.

> **Avis Rent-a-car** – vehicle rental
> **Holiday Inns** – hotels & catering

A major argument for franchising is that there is inherently **less risk** because others have already done the pioneering and you will have the support of the franchisor. Further, it can represent a stepping-stone to a full 'own-business' while you gain experience. The down-sides are that it requires the up-front investment in the franchise fee, the on-going royalty reduces the potential profits available, and you clearly have less autonomy in what the business does or sells, which may restrict your business expansion plans.

You should almost certainly not set out on this road if you have no knowledge at all of the market. You are likely to be trading with an organisation that carries substantial muscle and one that may be heavy-handed. You should take the best specialist advice available and talk with the self-regulatory British Franchise Association (BFA) before making your own judgement. Here is a broad-brush checklist from which to start.

- Work out what investment you can afford. Don't over-gear yourself. How much do you need to take out of the business? Too much can ruin the business.
- Do you have experience in the industry sector sufficient to operate successfully in it, and does the business suit you and your family?
- Check whether the franchisor is a member of the BFA.
- Research the franchisor fully – is it successful and can you obtain credible references?
- See if the franchisor itself runs any of its own franchises.
- Try to ascertain whether other franchisees are successful and meet existing franchisees, not only those offered by the franchisor.
- Compare the actual contract offered with one in a different franchise trade and beware of a contract that calls for too heavy a commitment at the outset.
- Enquire what follow-up support is provided by the franchisor.

- Take care that the contract offers you reasonable protection against others entering your geographic area.
- Obtain the opinion of your professional advisors and talk to the specialist advisors in your clearing bank and firm of accountants.
- Evaluate fully the information pack provided by the franchisor and don't ignore unwelcome information or advice from others.
- Have a specialist franchise solicitor check your agreement, especially the termination clauses.
- Evaluate the proposition realistically, practically, and objectively. Ban emotion from your decisions!

The British Franchise Association has an information pack, costing about £25.00, available by credit card (Tel: 01491 578050 during business hours) which will assist you to evaluate the proposition. Or visit **www.british-franchise.org** for a broad view of their activities and services.

8.8 Buying a business

Another way to start your 'own-business' is to buy an existing one. This approach raises some different questions, but the key personal issues are the same as for those starting anew. As stated earlier, the proposition differs for those seeking a main income from those looking for a secondary, support or hobby income, but if a main income – and especially if external funding is needed – you must now ask yourself:

- whether you expect the business to fulfil your life's expectations in terms of income, pension provision, and net asset enhancement.
- whether you have enough of the necessary skills to acquire and run it successfully, grow it, perhaps merge it, and one day to sell it.

You will already have appraised your skills and attributes and should now also obtain as much independent advice as possible (paid-for and free, industry expertise and entrepreneurial) on you, the business, the industry etc. Set yourself some sensible and comprehensive targets – and especially some 'go/no go' decision points on proceeding with decisions.

One thing you should allow for – then double – is the time taken to find, analyse and negotiate the 'right' deal. This is true whether you wish to buy a business outright or as part of an MBI or BIMBO (management buy-in or buy-in and buy-out). Invariably the time taken to conclude a deal is far longer than anticipated – 1 to 2 years is not uncommon for a major deal – and it may be prudent to find or maintain other employment to secure your income base while you search for the right deal. Don't let time pressures convince you to go for a less-than-good option.

It is perhaps important to point out that there are differences between buying the business and buying the company. If buying the company, it comes with all debtors and creditors, known and unknown; if buying the business, you may still be acquiring unknown debts.

For the nitty-gritty areas of the actual acquisition: here is an outline check-list, to which you will need to add many further points of detail:

- Are your professional advisors all fully briefed and supportive?
- Is your business plan in place and does it stand up to any questions and criticisms?
- What is the initial outlay, including professional fees, and what further investment will be required to make the business more fully operational?
- Can you raise the necessary capital in a satisfactory way? Are there other ways to finance the deal – e.g. by involving the vendor in a time-phased purchase?
- Do you know the particular trade or profession well enough?
- Do the statutory and management accounts look convincing?
- Has the business been successful and grown in recent years?
- What is the reason being given for its sale now? Do you believe it?
- What liabilities would you be taking on – e.g. staff and long-term trading contracts? This can contain some nasty surprises for example in pension or redundancy entitlements. The Transfer of Undertaking (Protection of Employment) 'TUPE' regulations will transfer to the buyer of a business the liability for employees, including those dismissed in anticipation of the sale (who may be able to claim unfair dismissal). Could you be liable?
- Are the assets fairly valued? In particular, have you reviewed the stock declared to see if it is saleable etc? Are there goods already on order which are not required?

- Is the value for any goodwill reasonable?
- Is the sale drawn up in a reasonably tax-effective manner – for you? This can be a major issue.
- Will the vendor give adequate warranties?
- Has the consideration been phased over a year or two so that any warranty claims can be enforced against the balance owing?
- Does the goodwill centre personally around the vendor? What happens when he goes? If he has offered to stay for a time, will he actually stay on once he has the money?

It will, of course, be expensive if a proposed purchase fails in the final stages. You will be well advised to enquire carefully about the level of professional fees you are incurring and to arrange a **'Heads of Terms' agreement** (on which you should take early legal advice) to try to prevent the vendor from making an unreasonable withdrawal. Remember that acquisition costs are not tax-allowable against revenue but can only be relieved against a future capital gain on disposal of the business.

Although this section has been largely filled with caveats, often a genuine sale reason exists and a fair purchase price can be struck. An existing business does have the advantage that you will not have to grow it to the size at which it can support you, during which time you are working against the clock. The cost of this is part of the purchase price.

Your professional advisors may be prepared to reduce some of your initial financial risk by putting some or all of their fees on a contingent basis; this is often the case with corporate finance advisors. Remember however that they are also profit centres and that lowering your financial risk in the event of an aborted bid will mean higher fees if the deal goes ahead. You may also find that Merger & Acquisition specialists will not charge you a fee, being retained by the business vendor; so be aware of the risks of being 'advised' by the vendors' advisors.

In passing, note that at some stage you may wish to sell the business to someone else. Your purchasing experience could prove very useful in the future!

8.9　Key points

- Before thinking about your options, consider carefully what you want to get out of the business (see Chapter 2). Then assess your business options (and other options?) against your objectives.

- Is it full-time, part-time, or shared with others?

- Prepare yourself long lists of questions – and briefly write up the answers as you go. Revisit frequently.

- .

- .

- .

9

Using the Internet

9.1 Introduction

Over the last few years, the internet has grown radically in size, in ease of use and, as a result, its use has become widespread. Rarely today will you find a serious business that does not have at least an email address or more often, its own website. The internet can be used for research into markets, products, and competitors; it can also be used for marketing, advertising and selling. It can be used to supply a product in its own right or as a new form of delivery. Many books have been and are being written on the internet, which you can and should consult, but this chapter seeks just to outline some uses of the internet and web for the smaller business.

9.2 Setting up

I don't intend to give a detailed guide on getting yourself connected for two main reasons (a) it would take more than the whole of this book to do the job properly and (b) as fast as it is written, it is out-of-date! I have touched briefly elsewhere on the need to set up your PC or IT system for your business use; the next essential step is connecting to an internet Service Provider or 'ISP'. Buy a small book on the subject if you are not familiar – high street newsagents/bookshops will have a selection.

Often, your new PC will come with the ISP software already installed with hundreds of free hours of usage (provided they are all used within the first month!). Key things to look for are (a) support (with a capital S!) (b) speed and quality of service and (c) reliability.

Whatever else you do, invest in virus protection software. Some strange people find it fun to destroy other people's files and software by creating/spreading viruses, while others will seek to perpetrate fraud or theft. The only ways you can protect against viruses and unauthorised access to your PC is through virus protection software, firewalls, anti-spyware software, and a good dose of sensible precaution with passwords etc.

Best of all, get a friend who is PC and internet literate to help you in your choices!

9.3 Research

The internet opens up a world of possibilities for research. It is now easy to search for information on any topic, anywhere in the world. If you have already searched for information using one of the well-known search engines such as **www.google.com**, you will know how easily you can generate an unworkably long list of materials.

The business of search engines is to help you find the information you need out of the millions and millions of pages of information published on the web. A search engine will have simple and more complex search routines, which enable you to conduct a 'rough' search (possibly yielding thousands of results) or more refined search criteria to sharpen the focus. Learning how to use search engines cleverly will save you significant time and make research much less frustrating. Search smarter, not longer, and use the 'advanced search' or 'power search' options.

9.4 Email/contact

Email has probably become the major form of communication and most new businesses are likely to find it an essential business tool. Before you get your new business cards/ brochure/ letterhead printed, you will need to decide on your email address.

Your ISP will probably offer you one or more email addresses – or you may have one already. Before you skip to the next section, consider what impact the address will have on your business image. An address such as 'john@bigears.co.uk' may cause amusement amongst your friends, or could be relevant if you specialise in supplies for donkey-lovers; it hardly helps an independent consultant's professional image. You may find that your desired address has already been taken, or that it is a 'low-priority item' but remember it will be one of the first things a potential customer will see – and you will need it on your stationery.

Treat your emails as you would any other form of communication in terms of prompt and courteous response, sensible filing systems etc. Email has some huge advantages over letters, e.g. the ability to group together customer addresses and then email special offers to particular interest groups with minimal 'postage' cost. (For information on anti-spamming legislation – see section 4.6(d)).

Before looking to the next section on marketing/advertising, which will require a material investment to be effective, first consider how to use emails for marketing.

9.5 Marketing and advertising

The internet has become widely used for marketing due mainly to its **accessibility** and the very **low marginal cost** of using it. In order to use the web for marketing, you will probably want to set up your own web-site. Similar comments apply as in email regarding the freely provided web-sites from your ISP and the need to consider carefully the name and image it creates. Having a web-site is no guarantee that anyone will visit it and there are industry specialists in how to attract 'hits' via search engines. If this in important to your business, it is almost certainly worth considering engaging such a specialist.

You will probably find too that the web needs some of the more 'old-fashioned' support like advertising your website in your corporate literature or possibly taking out a regular small advertisement in a relevant newspaper. More 'modern' support includes using links from related websites, banner ads, and getting good rankings on search engines using embedded meta-data.

Actions such as these can encourage people to visit your site once – it's then up to the site to draw them back. It's likely that you'll need to update your site regularly and often, and send out emails detailing some of the changes to people who have registered on the site and who could be interested in following up. Getting your potential customers to 'sign on' for a regular newsletter (or similar) can be a great way to keep a target list. It's also useful to keep in touch with your recent customers and clients. You must get people's approval for their names to be on your email list to avoid the accusation of 'spamming'. (See Section 4.6(d)).

It's a widely held belief that much (most?) advertising is wasted and the same can be true of websites. If you have ever waited a minute or so for detailed pictures or banners to load in order to access a website, you'll know how short the attention span is of the average website visitor. However, web advertising and (see the next section) selling/supply can take geography, size, and time out of your business – you could be supplying someone thousands of miles away or next door, and be open for business 24/7.

Think about the image you are creating and how it fits your intentions for the business. Have a look at your competitors – or just at other sites you find interesting and want to revisit. Hire a professional – preferably someone recommended and certainly someone whose sites you have seen and liked. Stand out as an interesting and relevant site.

Read *Marketing Your Business* by Martin Bailey, published by MB2000, for expert advice and ideas covering everything from this last section.

9.6 Selling and supply

The follow-on from bringing your product or service to the attention of customers is considering how to get them to buy over the net. The psychology of selling applies just as much to the net as anywhere else. Can you sell your product/service over the net? Should you do so? It may instead be a more valid option to use a phone call when customers want further information and then to take down credit card details for purchase.

If you set up to sell over the internet, your site will need to cater fully for the shopper – display, shopping carts, and anything else needed for an online shop. If you sell entirely on-line, you will have little need for premises, and storage and distribution may be minimal – and it is open all hours. In any event, as with retailing, you will need to set up the facility for customers to pay by credit card. The key difference about selling over the net is that the customer is not present and therefore has different rights regarding change of mind and accepting the goods – you will bear a greater risk. Talk to your bank specialists.

There are quite significant new legal requirements on you if you decide to trade over the net and you are well advised to talk to your lawyer about these requirements before committing yourself too heavily.

You need to make it easy for people to buy, in an environment that they find 'safe', although the whole area of the internet is often not seen as friendly.

9.7 Banking

Just a couple of sentences here. In the 'good old days', you had to go to the bank to do (almost) anything other than pay for something by cheque or credit/debit card. Telephone banking is a huge advance for the smaller business, but the emergence of internet and online banking has created the opportunity for smaller business to gain better deals, switch money around between interest and cheque accounts, and pay suppliers online. Does it represent a good deal for you?

9.8   Key points

- The internet is a massive resource which can save (or use up) a massive amount of time – and provide much assistance. Consider how best to use it.

- Refer to the library of good books, and to your friends and contacts, to 'bone up' before you start.

- The internet may need support from more traditional forms of market research, marketing, advertising, selling, and supply.

- Contact your local business support organisations to find out about free or subsidised training.

- .

- .

- .

10

Selling

10.1 Introduction

Having followed the guidance in Chapter 3 on marketing your 'own-business' effectively to bring you to the attention of a potential customer or client, you will need to move into selling mode to convert the client's initial attention into having a meeting with you, where you can start selling to gain firm orders or a contract. Different sales techniques may be used in the various situations encountered, and this chapter summarises some possible approaches, although it is focussed on significant, or higher value, sales. This may not be directly relevant to some retail situations, but some of the techniques discussed will still be useful.

Selling involves providing (a range of) goods and/or services to meet the client's needs, real or imagined, corporate or personal. The selling process is long and continuous. The process starts from during the first contact with your potential customer – be it a telephone call to set up the first sales meeting – and will cover developing your understanding of the client, the client's market and needs, defining the need, agreeing the solutions, meeting any objections, and closing the sale. There is a wide range of selling styles and techniques available; no one such technique or style will be suitable for all situations. You will need to stay flexible enough to recognise current requirements and adapt your current style appropriately.

The golden rule of selling is that **a sale is not completed until the goods/services are delivered and the money has been cleared to your bank account.** Promises and half-hearted commitments do not help you to stay afloat! Another useful definition I have heard is that 'selling is satisfying customer needs at a profit'. 'Satisfying customer needs' means meeting a pre-existing need, not selling something the customer doesn't want (although 'pre-existing need' can include a need that you generated earlier), and 'at a profit' needs little further explanation!

The process of gaining new business may be defined as:

1. finding the customer
2. gaining the first interview
3. sales meetings
4. selling benefits
5. dealing with objections
6. closing the sale.

Finding the customer – or marketing – was covered earlier; steps (2) to (6) inclusive are addressed below.

Another useful way of describing the sales processes is by using the acronym AIDA – meaning

> Gain the customer's **A**ttention
> Provoke **I**nterest
> Create **D**esire to buy
> Initiate **A**ction to close the sale

However, before moving on to talk about selling, one aspect often overlooked is the preparation required. You are about to embark on a process of building a relationship with a (potential) client. Almost everything you do will either enhance or spoil that relationship, and you don't want it to be affected by lack of forethought on your part. Examples of research you should be undertaking include:

- the background of your customers, their businesses, the markets in which they operate, and the competition.
- how your product/service relates to competitive offerings.
- simple things – like how to get to your customer's office!
- possible thoughts, concerns, objections, and how you might deal with them.

- how you want to tackle the sales process – alternatives – how you can 'regroup' if things start to go wrong.
- being prepared for every eventuality!

10.2 Gaining the first interview

10.2(a) Getting to meet

Selling is very much a person-to-person issue. You are most likely to achieve sales by convincing potential clients, in one or more face-to-face meetings, that their fears can be allayed, their ambitions realised, or their problems solved through your personal interactions with them. If you build personal relationships, they will help you overcome problems in decision-making based on logic; thorough logical analysis and preparation is also required, but it will not assist you overcome personal relationship objections.

You are extremely unlikely to be able to sell anything solely by telephone. However, your first contact with potential clients (other than by your marketing letters, advertisements or website) will be by phone and that contact will require selling skills to convert expressed initial interest into agreeing to a first meeting. This does not mean a 'hard sell', but the usage of specific telephone techniques.

General skills required for effective telephoning include:

- being well prepared with information on the client's company, its market, industry issues, specific problems you know the company has experienced and about which you know something useful etc.
- speaking clearly, concisely and pleasantly.
- concentrating on the client; listening to what is, and what is not, being said.
- good fact-finding when listening.
- effective note-taking.
- asking 'open' questions (i.e. those that cannot be answered with a simple 'Yes' or 'No' and that require the client to comment) or questions that require a positive response.
- smiling as you talk!

Specific sales skills that will be needed in selling all the way from the first meeting to the final 'close' include:

- preparation and practice
- setting your own sales targets – what do you hope to achieve at each meeting?
- a positive, friendly approach, sincerity and trust
- the skill of generating the client's interest in you – and your interest in your client
- not 'selling' the goods/service features but the benefits that will accrue to the client
- using examples of past successes
- subsequent analysis and improvement.

The only objective when you first speak to a client after your initial marketing contact is to **set up an early meeting** with the decision-maker (in the company). You need to establish, in your call, a clear and compelling reason for that decision-maker to meet you. If possible, you should also use any opportunity to gain as much information as you can about that person, the business, the industry and so on. Your approach to the contact will be geared to the client's response to your marketing, but always bear the above general points in mind. It is possible to cold-call, but this will be very time-consuming and is usually not very rewarding. If you do decide to approach a client 'cold' by telephone, you can perhaps allude to a possible benefit that you can deliver, e.g. *'You may be eligible for a grant'* or *'We have a special offer ...'*- which might increase your success rate.

Initially (at least) **prepare scripts** for your telephone calls, starting with the introduction, through to confirming the client's interest, the 'trial close' and the date to meet. Don't ask clients whether they want to meet you, but assume a meeting is beneficial to both of you – and ensure that it is! Seek a positive response to a choice of meeting dates. There is only one 'first time', only one chance to make a first impression, so don't waste it. **Identify the key issues** for discussion.

Your introduction will need to refer not only to who you are and why you are ringing, but also to the marketing mailing (or their response) that led to this telephone contact. You could refer directly to their response – or by asking the question *'Did you receive my letter...'* (If the answer to this is 'No', try to close the conversation with a promise to send the information; don't try to explain your message from a cold start). Consider, before the call, the likelihood that you might speak first to someone other than the decision-maker – and how that conversation might run. There are four potential barriers to overcome – the secretary or 'gatekeeper', voicemail, 'other people', and the client – prepare yourself for each. Be polite, positive and open in requesting the assistance of other people on the phone to reach the decision-maker, with a product or service to help.

Having reached the 'boss', can you lead the conversation into the possible areas of concern that you have identified? Decision-makers are often approached by sales people and are unfortunately well used to 'tacky' sales lines or pressure selling. Treat clients carefully and professionally, offering one genuine reason why the individual client should see you. Remember – be positive – all you are requesting is (say) a 30 minute meeting to explain the benefits of using your skills, product, or service. If you do ask for 30 minutes, keep your promise at no more than a half-hour meeting.

As an aid to positive selling, one author advises you to prepare a 'confidence card' to put beside your phone, saying:

- **I have valuable services that many non-clients need that will enable them to improve their operations.**

- **People are sometimes hesitant to make appointments over the phone. This does not mean they are rejecting me or my idea.**

- **I have succeeded before and I will succeed today!**

- **I have a perfect right and responsibility to discuss my services with eligible prospects.**

With acknowledgements to Dick Connor and Jeff Davidson's *Getting New Clients*, published by John Wiley & Sons Inc.

How do you handle objections at this stage – and turn the conversation back to a positive tone to allow you to set up a meeting? Script out the possible objections (and those you meet subsequently) with your possible answers, e.g.:

Objection: 'I'm really not interested in buying xxxxx.'

Answer: Your answer could start by mentioning some recent success, which you believe could be of interest, finishing with something like *'I will only need 30 minutes of your time.'* followed by a choice of meeting dates or *'When would it be convenient to meet?'*

or ...

Objection: 'I don't have time to meet.'

Answer: Along the lines of *'I don't want to waste your time, but I believe we can help your business growth because in some recent work we found that ... (something relevant to the business)'*, followed by a closing statement.

Whilst these are necessarily summarised and simplified conversations, they show some ideas for dealing with the initial objections. The words above will not be what you will actually say – but how would you deal with any similar objections in a positive way, a way that invites agreement to meet? Add your own variations, but always close by asking to meet.

Having agreed the appointment, **confirm it in writing.** Sometimes you will have to admit failure; in these cases, analyse what was said and how you might have won. Remember the 80/20 rule that 80% of your business will come from 20% of your clients – it may be necessary to lose some clients on the way, as it would take too much time to convert them to a sale or the likely business is very insubstantial. But, a 'No' today means you are one step nearer a 'Yes' in the future. Don't take the 'Nos' personally; there are bound to be some negative responses before getting to 'Yes', so get the 'Nos' over with.

10.2(b) The first meeting

Before any meeting you need to follow some basic rules such as – **prepare well**, arrive early, be alert and friendly, bring your business cards and brochures and all your materials. Preparation is never more necessary than for a sales meeting. Look back at the general points listed above and reflect how the initial impressions you offer convey the right sense of professionalism, the high level of trust and so on required. Be ready to observe all the verbal and non-verbal (body-language) signals of how the meeting is going. You only have one chance to make a first impression!

Think through your minimum/maximum price, other possible or likely issues, and how to resolve them, what is achievable in this one meeting, and how will you get there! What is it you want to gain from this first meeting – as a minimum, and as a 'best possible outcome'?

Listen well and encourage clients to talk about their perceptions of the major industry concerns and issues. Part of your job is to prompt the conversation flow from the initial introductions onwards. Only wait for a client to move if this is part of your plan – you are there to reduce tension and build trust, breaking down the barriers to open discussion. Long silences or disjointed conversation do not do this. Know what questions you want to ask to **identify the key client issues** and needs – issues or needs which will require your product/services. Try to establish some common ground with the client, either briefly at a personal level, or in more detail at business sector level. Establish the client's overall business and personal objectives and consider how you can help achieve them. Certainly at this first meeting do not criticise the client or the company, but perhaps suggest areas for attention, e.g. by saying 'I wonder if ...'

Once clients start talking, needs and worries will start surfacing – remember the 80/20 rule again in this case that you do 80% of the listening and 20% of the talking. Usually, the first meeting is about **building relationships** and fact-finding; it is unlikely to lead to a sale, or signing or agreeing the contract, but be prepared to do so if it does. Even if no contract ever emerges, information gained will build your store of knowledge to use with other clients. It also allows you to practise displaying your expertise, adding to your public profile; after all, the client could still become a source of referrals.

Establish early in the meeting that you are talking to the decision-maker. If not, you may be wasting your time, time better spent on convincing someone with the budget to spend on solving problems. In any organisation there is always someone responsible for the budget (in larger organisations, there may be several decision-making units). Find out how the business operates. If your contact is not at the right level, find out who is and try to move on to the right person, while retaining your initial contact as the 'product champion' or your 'this-business-mentor' inside the firm. Some people refer to this person as the 'MAN' – the one with the **M**oney, the **A**uthority and the **N**eed.

Be brief (check about any time limits the client has for the meeting) and businesslike, with the aim of closing the meeting by reaching an outline of what the client wants, or with the agenda and date of the next meeting. Try not to be drawn into a price discussion too early – emphasising that you need to understand the issues before defining the solution more clearly. This first meeting is about building a personal relationship with another professional and establishing the facts, so that you can work together later on the solutions.

10.2(c) When to quit

Perhaps a surprising heading at this stage, but there will be occasions when it would be better for you not to proceed to a sale with the prospect. Some of the situations where this could apply are:

- when the business has no cash and cannot afford to pay you
- when you have a strong personal dislike of the business or the individual
- you have serious doubts about the client's business ethics
- the business is genuinely outside your business competence. (Can you subcontract it?)

How you decline professionally will depend on the cause of your concern and on the client, but options would include pricing very high, setting a very long timescale 'because of the other outstanding work', or an honest 'no-can-do, but I know a man who can' – with a view to gaining future contracts. If you treat your contacts fairly and honestly, they will be more willing to talk to you again and more prepared for you to keep in touch.

10.3 Subsequent sales meetings

Subsequent sales meetings have a common purpose with the first meeting, i.e. continuing to **build on the initial personal relationship**. You want to develop this to the point where you are the natural choice.

The real selling starts in these later meetings and you need to be comfortable with your professional sales approach. Selling takes time and requires you to follow a planned approach of working out what is required, defining how you will meet this established need, the benefits accruing to the business – and then asking for the contract or sale.

Don't try to rush the decisions. Find out as much as you can about the issues and your customers' needs, any competitive proposals, budget constraints. Clarify at each stage what you have understood, to establish that you can meet the needs.

Develop the technique of **asking probing questions**, of an open-ended nature, requiring long explanatory answers from the client, questions which cannot be answered by a yes/no response, unless of course you want to close down an area of discussion and move on or change direction. Ask whether your understanding of the client's needs and priorities is correct and confirm that the approach offered will meet those needs. Understanding the issues now will make selling later that much easier. You need to be able to state where the firm/client is now and where they would like to be; if you can get them there, you will have completed the project.

Although you have prepared your approach, be ready to amend/alter your presentation as a result of responses your clients make to your questions. This shows that you really are listening – and are someone they can work with, not someone who presents ready-made 'one-size-fits-all' solutions.

After each meeting, make it a rule (which can however be broken when appropriate!) to confirm the up-to-date situation in writing to clients, but allow adequate time for them to think things over or 'stew'. All good ideas need a gestation period, long enough but not too long – you will need to recognise when to strike for the business. You will only get what you ask for, but will need to choose the right moment to ask.

10.4 Selling benefits

As I have already said, clients rarely buy totally objectively – they often **decide emotionally** and look for the benefits to them that purchase brings. You must therefore address this need by spelling out how, with your assistance, clients will reach their business or personal goals or cut out concerns etc. Verifiable reasons include: convenience, running costs, after-sales service, professional help, price advantage, special features.

You must talk about the problems they have identified, how your assistance can help **resolve them** and how you have helped in the past with other clients (with examples). You will, in the previous stages, have made sure you have understood the key issues affecting your clients and their businesses (these are not necessarily the same thing); for each client now you should prepare a written proposal for discussion, either as a draft proposal or just as a briefing note for you. You need to ensure that you are bringing something new, but any client contributions to them will start the 'working together' process.

Be prepared to talk through the proposed timescale and to present your price structure and payment terms, not as a cost, but as the (small) investment required in order to gain the (large) **benefits**. These benefits will need to be spelled out in clear precise terms, as close to an increase in profit or to problem elimination (= profit gain) as possible. The closer you can define the cash benefits, the easier you will make it for your clients to see how sensible it is to buy your services – *'After all, it's a small cost for such great benefits'.*

When defining the service that you will offer to meet the needs, link it to the benefits by saying something like:

'..., which means ...', or '..., which cuts costs by ...', or 'what this means to you is that ...'.

Listen well to everything said and implied (see below for dealing with objections). Have some relevant examples of previous work you have done in this area and of the benefits accruing to the decision-maker and/or his company.

Throughout the process, keep your eyes open for **further opportunities** – which *may* arise at a future date **if you do a good job now**. Be persuasive, but not 'over the top' and know your skill limitations.

10.5 Dealing with objections

If a client brings up a new objection, acknowledge it and deal with it quickly, don't waffle! However carefully you have carried out the initial finding-out phase, any client may have objections of which you were not aware and which were not established in the opening discussions – and which come back for the kill just as you are about to close the sale. Spend time away from the client imagining what client objections there could be and prepare written questions and answers with which you feel comfortable. Remember that objections can be buying signals from your client who is thinking *'If only I can overcome this issue, then I can initiate this contract to...'*

First, **acknowledge that the objections are valid** concerns. There is nothing as irritating as a salesman who brushes aside objections as irrelevant. Your client has the right to be worried at this new step. By acknowledging the concerns, you are not agreeing to the objections, you are continuing to say that the customer's concerns are important to you and that you will try to deal with them constructively.

Find out exactly what's worrying your client – until you do, you stand little chance of curing the problem. Stress that it's not a disagreement; it's moving towards agreement. Try to persuade your client to be specific for the same reason. Perhaps seek agreement that, if you can resolve that particular problem, you will be awarded the contract or, if this flushes out other problems, jointly prioritise the issues. Consider how to meet your client's needs and the effect on your business.

Until you have dealt with clients' objections to their satisfaction, you are very unlikely to close any sales. If objections are 'brushed over', they will come back to haunt you. If you have spent time convincing the client that you are professional and that a purchase commitment will bring benefits to the client or the firm, your client really will want you to solve those last-minute objections (possibly raised by colleagues) in order to get on with the project.

10.6 Closing the sale

Before attempting to close the sale, you must be sure that you have understood clearly what are the 'drivers' making your clients consider your services. You must also have presented the benefits they will derive from the purchase, in a way they fully understand, and you need to have dealt professionally with all objections and concerns. The decision to move from discussion to **purchase is an emotional decision**, but the client will need to **justify it logically** – internally and /or to peers inside the company. Your relationship-building will help the client make the decision, but you should have worked together on the logic of the decision and on the objections.

A good way of ensuring that the time is ripe is to **summarise** where your discussions started, the process the two of you have been through, your understanding of the key issues and priorities, together with your proposals for addressing them and the benefits accruing to the client when you have solved the problems. It will also be important to summarise how you have dealt with any concerns raised.

This summarising process restates and emphasises how the two of you have reached agreement on the solutions to the problems and should enable you to move into the closing process, i.e. the stage of obtaining agreement to purchase. It can be very helpful to use the 'trial close' process to see whether your client is ready to buy. The trial close is when you seek an opinion, as distinct from a sale close which asks for a decision. The trial close involves a statement such as *'I think we're getting close to agreement, aren't we?'* or *'I think our [ABC model] fits the bill, doesn't it?'* – which can generate a positive or negative response. If positive, reinforce the opinion your client has given and move in for a close. If negative, offer understanding of where the client is, the client's feelings or concerns, deal with them as described earlier, explain the benefits again, and seek to move in for a trial close (until the response to a trial close is positive!).

There are many ways of moving to the 'close' and a few of these are listed below. This is not an exhaustive list, but examples to show some alternative approaches.

Direct request   *'We seem to agree that I can assist in meeting these goals. If you give me the go-ahead, can I start/deliver on Monday next?'*

Assumption   *'We need to get moving quickly to ... I could start on ...'*

Alternative   *'Given my other commitments, I could either start on ... or on ... Which would be better?'*

| Conditional | *'If I can (resolve that issue), do we have a deal?'* |
| Provisional | *'Subject to the committee agreeing to your recommendations, when do we start?'* |

Never wait for your client to close – always ask for the order directly or in the form of an alternative close. Ask and then stop talking – the silence will help your client to focus – and further talking at this stage will divert attention away from the close process. Also, when you sense the time is ripe to close, stop 'selling' – or you may talk yourself and the client out of the sale!

Sometimes you will get a 'No' decision. Plan ahead how to deal with this and make your exit, leaving the door open for an early return. It could be that you have converted a good client who has other priorities presently, but who has been impressed by your presentation and who **will come back**.

10.7   Delivering the goods/service

All the steps you take when supplying your goods/services must be undertaken realising that the client is just that – a client paying for your specialist services. You must be selling at all times (hence the oft-used acronym 'ABS' or 'Always Be Selling'). Clients need to be told, regularly but not objectionably, that they have made a wise decision bringing in large benefits. Keep listening for other opportunities, but follow all the earlier advice about how you get to the sales 'close'.

10.8   Retaining clients

Your best customers are usually your existing ones. Yet the majority of your customers will leave you in time. Why? According to research, the main reasons that customers move away are that 10% move because of price, 10% are natural complainers who are never satisfied, 10% for 'other' reasons, and 70% because the supplier 'does not care enough'. No business can afford to lose customers, yet look at the last time you had bad service, how did you feel? The main reason for customers leaving is lack of care and attention by the business which is supposed to be servicing them!

I have referred earlier to the need for a customer database to enable you to make special offers or whatever to meet individual customer preferences. Keep your database up-to-date at all times – it is the route to the lifeblood of your business – customers. As well as 'tombstone' information (name, contact details, demographics etc) include what they bought, when, information on their business, industry etc. (NB Data Protection registration – see Section 4.5)

Remember too that it is radically cheaper to retain an existing or past customer than to find and convert a new one. Regular or repeat customers cost less to serve and can be a good source of recommendations or referrals to new ones.

Future contacts you make with them must all emphasise the importance of your customers to you – whether it is the way your telephone is answered, how problems are addressed, or promises delivered. Make your clients 'important people'; remember business and personal details about them, what makes it easy and rewarding for **them to do business with you**. Keep in touch.

Doing 'enough' is no longer enough. You will need to develop a customer-focused approach right through your business dealings. From the first point of contact to follow-up care, focus on their point of view. If customers complain – over-deliver on your response; it improves your service, stops them complaining elsewhere about you, and may even impress them. Seek feedback from past clients/customers with a genuine wish to implement good ideas. Much is said today about 'relationship marketing' – another phrase for looking after real people in a personal way.

Do that little bit extra – it might just beat off the competition.

10.9 Keep selling!

A wide discourse on selling is outside the scope of this book, but it is important to recognise how hard many people – even professional sales people – find the process of selling. It often feels like a direct personal rejection when a customer says 'No' and we all have to find ways to deal with that effectively, because sure as anything, there are more 'Nos' than 'Yesses' in life!

One model that I have found very useful in tackling this issue (I can't attribute it as the author seems now lost in the mists of time!) is the concept of a sales cycle, where each contact with the customer improves the chances of a sale.

So, the first step on the ladder is the first contact. Whatever the responses from the potential customer, even if an outright 'No', that potential customer will now have heard of you and is therefore more advanced in a potential relationship with you than before in the cycle.

You could think of it as progressively moving the potential customer up an incline towards a sale with each contact you make (whether mail, phone, face-to-face etc) viz:

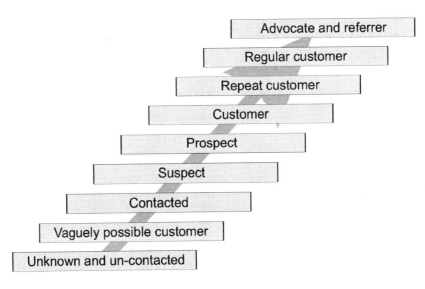

Now clearly you can put in as many (or as few) stages as you wish in the chain, but the concept of gradually moving potential clients uphill towards a sale is one that many have found a useful spur to keep on selling!

10.10 Key points

- Plan your approach to selling – and get some sales training if you think you might just need it.

- Preparation for sales meetings is vital; so is subsequent learning from experience.

- Listen 80% and talk 20%. Don't rush.

- In selling, you get what you ask for. One of the main pitfalls for new business-people is that they are unable to close the sale and so keep talking to potential clients for too long. Set up your own targets for moving through the sales process and stick to it well.

- You are the salesman, the sales manager and the MD and must act appropriately in all roles. If you cannot sell, you should not be in business on your own! Practice makes perfect, so keep at it.

- Look after your 'hard-won' customers.

- Be prepared to drop clients who do not pay, pay late, or at low rates, potential clients who will not commit to engage your services or buy products within a reasonable time, or marketing methods that do not deliver.

- Don't give up!

- .

- .

- .

11

Contracts

11.1 Introduction

Contracts – oral or written – govern many transactions in our lives. Most businesses will need to consider their contractual terms – not only for the day-to-day operations, but also, unfortunately, for those occasions when suppliers or customers don't live up to their side of the bargain. It's not that you will be taking people to court every day, but you may need to consider what terms to put in place for the odd occasion when 'needs must'.

11.2 Sales contract terms and conditions – or not?

In most businesses, contracts can be set up between your business and your customer. There are essentially two valid but opposing points of view with regard to formal contracts for goods to be delivered or work to be done, one being that contracts are essential, the other suggesting that seeking a formal contract will very materially reduce your chances of selling to a client. The basic arguments seem to run as follows.

For having a contract
The reasons for having a contract largely seem to be for your benefit as the supplier – although there may be some client benefits.

The main argument is that with a contract in place, both parties will be clear on the scope of work to be done or product to be supplied, the timescales and the costs involved. All the 'fringe benefits' to each are clearly and unequivocally stated and, in the event of a problem, both sides 'know where they are'. It is normal business practice to have 'Terms and Conditions' and both parties are ethical and wish to deal with matters professionally – therefore a contract is essential.

You will feel secure that the client cannot easily walk away and refuse to pay and you are also sure of what you have to deliver; your clients are sure they know what they are going to get, when, and how much it will cost.

You may also be able to limit your liabilities (to the extent allowed by law), set out the basis on which prices may be increased (or further charges made), and you may use the signing of the contract to 'close the sale'.

Against having a contract

From the client's point of view, the contract itself could be quite daunting, incorporating many terms and conditions to consider (which may never arise in practice) and which may put the client off completely. Thoughts may turn to what happens if you or the goods/services turn out to be not up to par, if you cannot complete on time, if there is a personality clash or some other problem. A detailed contract and terms of business will probably force the client to consider the full implications on day one, together with the full costs to be incurred – to which the client may not be prepared to commit, not having seen any of the benefits. The client may feel that someone who requires a detailed contract to provide a guarantee of payment is not worth engaging.

You may feel it better to start work and gradually persuade the client to purchase from you again – and then again – on an informal basis.

Conclusion

You must consider, from the point of view of the requirements of your business and of your own relationship with the client, which of these arguments feels more comfortable and therefore whether you wish to go down the route of having a formal contract – or not. You may find that with some clients you require a contract but that with others you prefer to operate on a handshake. Either way, read on!

11.3   Operating without a contract

Even if you do not wish to have a formal contract (and here comes the contradiction!) it is still worthwhile writing down a brief 'Heads of Agreement' document setting out the bones of what you have agreed, the basis on which you will send an invoice and get paid, and the timescales. Consider all the points in Section 11.4, but the wording of your 'Heads of Agreement' should be as simple and non-legal as practicable. Send or give your note to the client confirming that the attached 'outline' or 'project' is what you have agreed. Apart from client/consultant clarification, if you did fall out with the client, such a document might be very useful to your lawyer. Note that it is likely to be legally binding unless you expressly provide otherwise.

It is often useful to prepare non-legally binding Heads of Agreement (which should be clearly marked as such (see next paragraph)) as an aid to negotiation and full legally binding documents.

The phrase *'These Heads of Agreement are subject to contract and are not legally binding [ ]; they are prepared as an aid to the negotiation of formal legally binding documentation proposed to be agreed between us'* can be used to confirm this. If desired, the phrase *'with the exception of paragraph number [ ], [confidentiality]'* could be inserted after 'legally binding' to confirm that [the confidentiality clause] is binding. You can decide which, if any, clauses need to be where I have shown the square brackets.

11.4   Developing a contract

Let us assume you have decided that a formal contract is for you and that you have gone through the Heads of Agreement stage set out above and are now deciding what should be included in your contract. One useful way of proceeding is to separate the contract into two parts, being 'Terms of Business' and 'Conditions of Contract', the former being the terms that relate to this particular project and the latter being more the general contract conditions.

I have set out below some 'Terms of Business' and 'Conditions of

Contract' which may be appropriate – but check on the terms used by others in your sector. Both vary widely and you are responsible (subject to the comments in the immediately following section) for choosing what is relevant and appropriate.

11.4(a) Terms of Business

There are a number of headings that can be included under Terms of Business, which would include:

The Parties:	Your name/company name and client's name (and the phrase 'referred to herein as 'The Client'').
The Goods/Services to be provided:	This could be general goods/services to be provided over a period of time, or alternatively a detailed specification.
Duration and Timescales:	For consultancy or services rendered, an estimate of the days per month or overall days required for the project, the start date and finish date. You may wish to include a minimum period and a notice period for termination in the case of an on-going advisory service. For goods and/or services, order/delivery timescales. For any report(s) to be submitted, outline the content. Set out any materials to be prepared or meetings required.
Prices/Fees:	This should cover the commitment fee if any, sale price of goods, daily time charges, expenses, on-costs, and (for special consultancy projects) any 'success-related fees'. For defined projects, it would be appropriate to include a total cost figure.
Settlement:	When do you invoice and when are invoices payable?
Special Contract Terms:	Any particular contractual terms covering, for example confidentiality, availability of information, payment of special expenses etc.

Exclusivity: Is it important to ensure that you are the only person offering this service?

Cancellation/Termination: You may wish to impose particular cancellation provisions beyond those in the standard terms.

Standard Terms & Conditions: A statement that these are attached.

Confirmation of Acceptance: The final clause should contain a paragraph something like:-

I hereby accept the terms of business outlined above and in the attached Conditions of Contract on behalf of XXX Limited *(i.e. your client)*.

signed.................................... (authorised signatory)

date.......................................

11.4(b)   Conditions of Contract

A typical range of headings to be covered in the conditions of contract includes

1. **Definitions** – to define the words used in this Conditions of Contract.
2. **Interpretation** – legally defining how the headings etc are to be understood.
3. **General** – noting that these Conditions of Contract apply to all contracts between you and your client and that any qualifications to these Conditions of Contract must be mutually agreed and agreed in writing by you.
4. **Formation of contract** – any pre-conditions e.g. client's written acceptance, before the contract comes into effect.
5. **Completion of project.** You will give estimates of completion dates, but you may need to protect yourself against force majeure and the fact that timescales are estimates, but also confirm that you will use all reasonable endeavours to complete on time. You should specify that time is not of the essence, unless of course you have agreed that it is and have charged accordingly. Note that if time is of the essence and you fail to meet the deadlines, the other party can repudiate the contract and claim damages. Time may be implied to be of the essence (unless expressly excluded) e.g. by agreeing to a schedule of dates by which

things have to be delivered.

6. **Suspension of work**. If relevant, you may need to add on to your project timescales any periods you cannot work because the client's factory is on strike or suffering a similar suspension of work.

7. **Ownership**. When does ownership in the products pass to the clients? Who owns any intellectual property rights arising from the project? Do you wish to make specific provisions in case you wish to use any of the information (that which is not confidential) or product developments (not proprietary) gained during the contract elsewhere?

8. **Confidentiality**. What restrictions are there on information you have gained? Can you talk about the results of the project, indeed about the project itself? Will you offer confidentiality (what are the problems for you in 'plying your trade' elsewhere?). Can you refer to the client as a 'past client' in your published material? Does the fact of raising the question at all cause problems?

9. **Exemptions from liability and/or limitations to liability**. Whilst you will use all due care in completing the contract, what liability are you prepared to assume, what guarantees/warranties do you give, what limitations on your liability do you wish to impose (subject to any legal requirements)?

10. **Speed and quality of service**. Do you want to confirm that you are responsible for these and that you will deal diligently with any complaints?

11. **Prices, fees and expenses**. Perhaps a brief explanation of what you charge for? Is VAT applicable? Any general exceptions requiring client's prior approval etc?

12. **Payment**. A statement that invoices will be issued, on what timescale, and must be paid in accordance with the terms of business; if not, what compensation will you require?

13. **Prices**. What is your basis for increasing prices and what notice period will you give?

14. **Termination**. What gives you and/or the client the right to terminate the contract e.g. insolvency, liquidation, bankruptcy, non-payment of invoices, take-over? What is the notice period etc for 'normal' termination and what arrangements for outstanding work/deliveries when termination notice is given?

15. **Additional work**. What is to be done about work which is not included in the terms of business?
16. **Delegation of work**. Can you take on other staff to do the work?
17. **Client duties**. Your rights of access to information and people, support from the client and his advisors/staff, cooperation of same.
18. **Arbitration**. What arbitration mechanism (if any) do you wish to invoke? Is it for technical issues only or also for legal disputes?
19. **Notices**. Where should notices be served and how?
20. **Applicable Law**. This will generally be English Law and English Courts.

11.5 Purchase contracts

Many of the comments above apply in reverse in dealing with your suppliers. There is nothing to stop you from seeking to operate with or without contracts with your suppliers – subject to their agreement however.

Possibly a significant area of difference for you in this new venture will be the suppliers who insist that their terms of business will be the ones that apply to the transaction. This is commercial pressure and can, in some circumstances be resisted. If you have, for example, a unique product or service, you may be able to require your own terms to be used. This may a case of working with your contact inside a firm to discuss how to deal with his purchasing department.

11.6 Professional advice

If you decide to enter into contracts with clients and/or suppliers (and even if you decide a contract is not worth pursuing), it is virtually essential that you receive proper professional advice from a good commercial solicitor. You will appreciate that solicitors work on a time charge basis and clearly any work you can do in preparing rough drafts of your conditions of contract and terms of business will be helpful. However, remember that any agreements already reached with the client may require your lawyer's assistance to renegotiate if these impose unnecessary obligations on you. It is important therefore to engage your lawyer at the appropriate time.

11.7 Key points

- Prepare drafts of contracts etc before seeing your lawyer – but see your lawyer before showing the contract draft to the client.

- Undoing a poor contract is probably more expensive than seeking early advice.

- A simple contract is often better than nothing at all.

- .

- .

- .

12

Independent Consultancy

12.1 Introduction

Many people move into independent consultancy (including the similar career options of professional services, interim management, and freelancing) after being employed and many return to employment subsequently. If you are considering consultancy as your route to independence, it is critical to your success that you plan your entry to this new market area carefully and ensure that you have covered as many as possible of the adverse factors that could affect you. This chapter sets out some key aspects you will need to consider and, as before, it is aimed at full-time, main income consulting. If your purpose is to generate some part-time income to add to a material pension or other income, adjust the recommendations of this chapter to suit your aims.

12.2 Commercial issues

Regular surveys by one independent group of consultants have shown that over 65% of self-employed consultants return to employment in due course and only about 20% of established consultants bill over £50,000 pa, with between 33% and 50% billing less than £30,000 pa. (Note that **billings do not equal earnings**; earnings are billings after costs and overheads have been paid). Reasons given for the return to employed status include the comfort and security of employment, consultants who cannot or will not sell, and inadequate market research and marketing and, probably the most important, an inability to describe succinctly the service being sold. Another area of difficulty is that in many a 1-3 person firm, consultants need to be able to **do everything or anything** required; many people planning to go into independent consulting have ceased to 'do', they now 'manage'. Managing and generalist consulting are difficult to sell.

Generally speaking, 40% to 50% of an independent consultant's time will be spent actively selling and marketing, i.e. only a maximum of 50-60% of working time will be engaged on billable work, which has the effect of necessarily increasing fee rates significantly – the 5-day week that is worked has to be earned in 2½-3 days. However, most self-employed consultants rarely have the luxury of a 5-day week; it's usually a week of seven long days of long hours – at least for the first year or two. I believe this applies even to those seeking to establish a long-term part-time career; it takes significant effort to start a new business.

If you are to market your services effectively, you must ensure that the benefits to the client of engaging your services are obvious. For someone who has left a large organisation, where skills were 'taken for granted', the move into independent consultancy (i.e. personally selling one's own skills against an invoice) brings a radically different situation. Clients do not assume latent skills nor do they want to buy consultancy – they buy lower costs, higher sales, removal of problems, better quality etc. They do not necessarily recognise the need for assistance and will need to be persuaded to commit resources to employ external skills. Furthermore, clients will have preconceptions about consultants, such as that the costs entailed will be far higher than the benefits gained, which you will need to counter. Another related factor is that there are few general problems requiring general consultants – it is easier to sell specialist skills, therefore you need to become, be, or seem to be, a specialist and to do this you need to know your speciality.

A large survey carried out by a firm of consultants showed that, of companies approached who were not using consultants, 30% found them too expensive, 5% said they were too successful to need them and 65% said consultants were not relevant to their situation. This means that **in 95% of cases, consultants had been unable to demonstrate benefits or relevance**. You need to be able to show, enthusiastically, that your specialist skills are both beneficial and relevant!

Analyse your own strengths and weaknesses using any techniques and assistance available to you. Douglas Gray's book (see Appendix I) has a chapter dealing with the skills required for consultancy and careful analysis will help you define your areas of specialisation.

Strengths could include your personality, credibility, reputation, location (i.e. availability) and years of experience as well as any specialist technical expertise. In defining your strengths, be aware that you will need to sell your current strengths, not those you had several years ago. Perhaps you have ceased to be a practitioner of the skill – having been a manager too long.

Analyse your **weaknesses** and decide how to offset for technology, staffing, low budgets, lack of consultancy experience etc. remembering that weaknesses are rarely, if ever, counterbalanced by low pricing. Ways of off-setting weaknesses include setting up informal networks of other independent consultants (to support overloads or provide additional skills), or subscribing to databases for additional information sources, and/or regular personal training.

At the same time, review the **marketplace** for strategic or structural changes that could provide opportunities for you or for potential clients. You will need to define the boundaries of your niche or specialist area, the boundaries of your niche market being defined by technical and/or geographic areas, or customer types and sizes. The more clearly defined your market, the better targeted your marketing can be. You also need to know that sector well enough to discuss it easily and with confidence. Who are the main players in the sector, the rising stars, technology trends, international movements, companies serving the sector etc? Practise being first of all a source of information, secondly an advisor and confidante, and lastly a salesman and consultant.

Understand and be able to describe your **expertise** easily. Bear in mind too that having defined these carefully, you may also wish to create business expansion opportunities by extending the service offered by organising extra training for yourself, or by bringing in associates or simply by competently undertaking a project to relieve a client concern and using your general business skills. You cannot be 'all things to all men, all the time' but neither should you be so specialised that there is rarely a job for your talents.

Your office **image** will include the need to set up retrievable filing, research facilities (on- and off-site), as well as the image given by the information conveyed in your standard letters and proposals etc – is it professional? As an example, unless either you or your partner is sufficiently expert, it may be sensible to sub-contract your typing to a local bureau or service.

Mailings are of little use unless followed up shortly after by a phone call (within 7 days), so batch your mailings to enable you to cope with the demands of the follow-up. Use the telephone contact primarily to set up meetings and to pre-qualify potential clients; don't try to sell consultancy over the phone, **it does not work**. Selling takes place on a face-to-face basis, especially in consultancy, and you will need to develop both telephone and selling skills to convert interest generated by marketing into paid projects. Even at this stage, however, you will need to prepare carefully for your telephone approaches, with scripted questions and answers plus practice beforehand and notes, analysis of results and development subsequently, with the sole purpose of improving your skill and success at gaining interviews.

Indirect marketing assistance can be gained by joining one of the major consultancies as an associate consultant, to be called on as and when appropriate business is gained. Large firms do engage associates where genuine specialist skills exist. It is also possible to enter into similar arrangements with smaller firms (or other sole traders) where services are complementary. In any such case, you should expect to receive only a proportion (say 35-60%) of the fees you generate, the balance being retained by the lead consultant. Their charges, and their support levels, vary widely from firm to firm and your percentage of the total is not necessarily a guide to their levels of effective support.

Interim management

A word or two about interim management – which sounds very attractive to former managers. (I distinguish interim management from consultancy by saying that if you want an interim manager, you know what you want to do, and you just don't have the person; if you want a consultant, you are not sure of what you want to do – even if you had the right person). If you are seeking interim management contracts, these are likely to be thin on the ground. They last (usually) for a longer term (say 3-6 months) and generally are offered at a somewhat lower fee rates than consultancy. Whilst there are agencies specialising in matching interim managers with assignments, most people find that there are far, far, more willing managers than projects. It is safe to assume that, even if you register with specialist agencies, you will have to generate most of your assignments yourself. This calls for effective marketing.

Consultancy franchise

One special form of agency which is on the increase is the consultancy grouping or franchises. There are a number of such firms, where the franchise fee or joining cost ranges from £250 to many thousands, where the percentage that the organisation charges you can range from 0% to 65% of your fees, and the services provided by the organisation extend from high to zero. Don't make any assumptions – it may be that you will be doing 100% of the marketing of your services and receiving 50% of the fees. Check to your own satisfaction what you will receive for your investment and whether or not the organisation is for you. As a minimum, you should meet the organisers of the group and some of the present franchisees – and not just the ones introduced to you by the group organisers.

Case histories

After completing successful assignments, develop an anonymous case history of each showing the process from problem identification, through to benefits achieved. These become powerful aids to future marketing, either through mailings or for use in face-to-face discussions.

How much time?

Many consultants start in business thinking they will be paid for working 5 days per week for about 48 weeks per year. Some will want to be paid for, say, 100 days and only work for 100 days. I'm sorry – it doesn't work like that in most cases! Initially at least, you may be working six or seven days per week for 50+ weeks, but many days will not be on a 'paid for' or chargeable basis. Apart from holidays, sickness, training and bank holidays, you will be actively engaged in unpaid marketing, sales and administration activities. Even when established, it is not uncommon to have only 100 – 120 paid days per year – which equates to a 50 – 60 % overall utilisation. To start with, use 110 working days as your benchmark to plan the business and for working out your fees.

Note that when fully up-and-running as a consultant, I believe that about 66% of your business should be targeted to come as repeat business from your existing client base as this improves utilisation – it's not a 'once-off' business.

Fees

The daily chargeout rate equivalent to your previous salaried remuneration is probably roughly equal to your last salary divided by 110; this represents a higher end daily rate but allows for 2 -2½ days paid work and 2½ – 3 days sales, marketing and administration per week. If you are offered a longer term 'full time' consultancy for a period of say 3 to 6 months, your client could technically argue for a 40% reduction in fee rate as you will be working 5 days not 3 days per week. (His view is that £500 for 3 days per week = £300 per day for 5 days per week.) However, when the project finishes, any marketing you had earlier initiated will be dead and you will be starting again with a new marketing plan, which will take time to have effect. You must allow for this unpaid marketing and the time taken (to restore the market positioning of your business) in your daily rate for longer term projects. In view of this, the maximum discount you can allow for longer term projects is probably about 20-25% of your full daily rate, i.e. dropping a £500 rate to £400 or perhaps £375.

As a general rule, you should not opt for fixed price contracts until you have much more experience of your time commitment to projects. Neither should you work for free – it makes it difficult to move to a professional, paid basis later. If you need to offer a 'freebie' or reduced price, see what other benefits you can derive from it – such as a positive written recommendation to another potential client.

Contingent fees, i.e. those that depend on success, can be a useful way of selling some services. They can also carry drawbacks by giving you divided loyalties 'I only get paid if I deliver a deal' can lead to 'Do I deliver the best deal for the client – or any deal at all, so long as I get paid?'.

Ten key features to aim for in marketing your consultancy successfully are:

1   Establish and know your competence in a limited and sensible range of skills.

2   Be able to define your competence, on paper and orally, to clients in a way that sells benefits not features. Practice your delivery. It's benefits to the client that win business.

3   Train continuously to improve and develop skills – to remain at the leading edge of (or at least up with) the industry. Read trade or professional journals regularly and thoroughly.

4   Research the available marketing processes (brochures, literature, mailings, PR, networking etc) to get you in front of decision-makers. Choose a working mix and implement it well. Monitor results and stay flexible.

5   Keep your eyes open for opportunities to sell your expertise. Be focused, yet flexible.

6   Manage the feasts and famines; neglect neither the work nor the marketing.

7   Use any available assistance, but don't expect other people to find paid assignments for you.

8   Concentrate on network contacts who can recommend you, or on others who can speed up the client conversion process.

9   Classify the clients you retain. Suggested categories – 'unknowns' are contacted and developed into 'prospects' and then into 'clients' through effective marketing and selling. Income flows from 'short-term clients' but significant income comes from repeat business from 'regular clients' or 'long-term clients' who form your 'AAA' list. 'AAA' clients will also recommend you to others, allow you to develop your sellable skills and to offer additional services. They should be nourished.

10) I'll repeat a tip from the chapter on sales: be prepared to drop clients who do not pay, pay late or at low rates, potential clients who will not commit to engage your services within a reasonable time, or marketing methods that do not deliver. Your resources are limited, filter the clients, concentrate on success.

In summary, **see it from the client's side of the desk**. It looks different from over there!

12.3 Tax issues

Many believe that the act of setting up in self employment as a consultant/subcontractor/freelance/interim automatically means that both Tax and NI will be based on the self-employed rates if they set up as a sole trader; alternatively that their personally-owned service company, which employs them, will be treated as an independent limited company (which can then decide how much to pay them under PAYE). This is not necessarily so.

There are a number of 'tests' applied by Revenue and Customs to prevent employees setting up as subcontractors to abuse the system and they allow the lower tax and NI only to those who, in their view, qualify. If you are genuinely self-employed, the advantages of these lower rates accrue mainly to you, but there can be some benefit also to your client company. The current legislation is set out on the Revenue and Customs website (**www.inlandrevenue.gov.uk**. or **www.hmrc.gov.uk**) and is usually referred to colloquially as the 'IR35' legislation. Be very aware of some of the most common pitfalls that could 'disqualify' you.

(a) If it were not for the intervention of your own limited company that employs you, would you be an employee of your client(s)? If so, the 'IR35' rules apply and however you set yourself up, your company's fees will be **taxed as if they were your earnings** and your company will have to account for PAYE and full employee's and employer's NI). This applies whatever proportion of your income you decide to pay as salary or dividends or keep in the company.

There are similar rules regarding sole traders – if you are really an employee, even part-time, full tax and employer/employee NI will be levied.

(b) The business should be able to make profits in good years, but will also have the risk of making losses through lack of work or through poor management decisions.

(c) Ideally, you should have more than just one client, although one client in the initial months may be justifiable.

(d) You, as the consultant, should be able to say where, when, and how, the services provided by you will be carried out.

(e) You should be required to provide all of your own equipment to carry out the services.

(f) Ideally, you should be able to subcontract-in other staff to assist (or replace) you in supplying the services. It is helpful if you employ others in your business.

(g) If you enter into a contract regarding the services you supply to your client – which is generally advisable – do **get a solicitor to review the terms** (inter alia) with employment/self-employment classification in mind. The terms and conditions you agree with your client as part of the contract should not be those typical for an employee, e.g. you should not be provided with a company car, nor should you be a member of the client company pension scheme. It follows therefore that consultancy for your former employer can present particular difficulties as well as opportunities.

(h) Your fees should, as far as possible, be based on projects done and on days/hours worked, rather than regular monthly sums. Your daily rate should be set high enough to allow for holiday pay/sick pay; these items should not be itemised separately in your invoice as they are your responsibility.

(i) Your consultancy advice should be available to all companies/individuals without restriction; the more restrictive your contract with a client, the more it appears to be an employment contract (apart from very necessary and acceptable restrictions on confidentiality).

(j) Supervision and/or direction by the client over you increases the implication of employment.

(k) Any indemnity given to your client regarding PAYE, VAT and/or NI should not form part of the contract to supply services.

(l) In all correspondence with the Revenue and Customs, and Social Security, do refer to your occupation as 'your business' rather than your earnings/income. Run the business in a professional manner, from record keeping to office facilities and printed business cards/stationery etc. Be prepared for an inspection of your premises, albeit your office at home, by any of the authorities.

(m) Remember that evasion of tax or non-declaration of earnings and/or non-payment of NI is illegal. There are many ways in which the authorities can check whether you are providing them with full information and the penalties for non-compliance can be extremely severe.

(n) Note that, if your earnings are merely 'casual' rather than part of an organised business, you cannot get your expenses set against your income for tax purposes; the rules for tax deductability are more restrictive in these circumstances. You can commence in business on a 'casual' basis, but once you feel it is a 'going concern', you should finalise it into a business format and advise the authorities accordingly.

Note that most of the 'rules' about self-employment set out above are 'strong indicators' rather than absolute rules; it is possible to fail some and still be considered self-employed. Seek advice from your accountant on the current legislation on this issue.

12.4 Key points

➤ Independent consultancy is not the 'easy option' some think it is.

➤ Be clear on the benefits you can bring to the client – and be able to talk convincingly about them.

➤ Pricing down is not a good sales strategy. Better to sell benefits effectively and satisfy your clients.

➤ Telephone selling of consultancy doesn't work – it's a face-to-face sale.

➤ Beware of the tax issues, especially if working for a former employer.

➤ Manage the feasts and famines; neglect neither the work nor the marketing.

➤ Use others to help your marketing, but don't expect anyone to find you work.

➤ .

➤ .

➤ .

13

Retailing

13.1 Introduction

Many people will see their future in opening a small shop or restaurant as their 'own-business'. Retailing is one of the hardest markets to work in, with issues like competition from major store chains to be addressed. There are still opportunities, even if the margin for error is small. Many issues facing such a new business are similar to any start-up in any sector, but this chapter addresses some issues which have different or greater importance for retailers.

13.2 Type of business

The first decision you will need to make – maybe you have already made it – is what type of business you are going to start. 'Retailing' covers a huge range of options including: convenience stores, specialist foods, non-food, sports goods, electrical, licensed goods, CTN (confectionery, tobacco, newsagents), in fact any store you can see on your high street or other location. This business is going to take up a major part of your life, so you'd better like it and be prepared to become an expert in it! Take time when researching the market to think about the effects on you and your family.

In retail especially, nothing is static. Your assessment today of the market, economy, business trends, fashion will set out some of the main issues for establishing your business, but how can they be changed – possibly at short notice – to accommodate changes occurring in the economy, the market etc? Is the business one that will keep you 'charged up' for as long as it will take you to establish, grow, and possibly sell a business? Will you have to 'live over the shop' and how will that affect you and your family?

Key issues for retailers are:

- 'location, location, location'
- full market understanding and knowledge
- understanding customers' buying motives
- keeping and using good records
- recruiting and managing the right staff
- commitment to the business
- being financially aware
- having relevant specialist skills
- and – remembering that cash is not the same thing as profit.

Possibly no other business sector has a greater requirement for business planning – **before** you start out in your new venture. Costs can escalate out of control in the retail business very quickly and give you no time at all to recover. Planning – and then doing some 'what if' analyses – if the sales are 20% down, then if it takes twice as long, then if the start-up costs are 100% higher, then if … Planning for it does not mean expecting it, rather being prepared for the possibility with an action plan should it occur.

13.3 Premises

One of the first decisions most 'own-business' retailers will have to take is 'Where do I locate?' Location is also possibly one of the greatest decisions and one where the effects of poor decisions can be large and fatal. **Location is always important**, but rarely more so than when the business relies on people 'passing by' for its business, especially where the purchase is not a distress purchase (i.e. one which just has to be made right now). Having the wrong location may well require significant (and possibly unsuccessful) changes in your product/price/range/promotional mix to compensate – which is always likely to be expensive, even if successful.

As part of your initial market research, you will have identified who your customers are likely to be and the ways in which you will attract them to come to you. Before committing yourself in any way to a shop in a particular area or street or building, consider how the location issues might affect your business. At the most obvious level, can they find you? Different areas/districts can have completely different buying patterns which could radically affect your stock policy – whether it's about clothes or food or PCs. What can you learn about the area – visit it to see, for example, if and when it's busy, the type of shops/businesses, the types of customers. Consider – will people travel to visit you, what's the competition locally, what will draw people in – in addition to your fantastic offerings! If your business is mainly focussed on female customers, would it be helpful to be close to other similar or related shops – or close to a male-focussed retailer? What about access, car-parking, convenience, neighbours, space? How much of your business relies on 'passing trade'?

I have referred elsewhere to taking out leases, but don't forget the possibility of a negative premium to persuade you into the premises – and also consider the reasons why it might be available. Try to avoid taking shop premises which are away from main trading areas, e.g. in basements, second floor with limited access etc. Settling on your premises is definitely not a decision to be taken quickly or lightly. Become familiar with the area before committing yourself to a lease or rental.

In terms of fitting out your premises – get professional assistance unless it really is an area of your expertise. Try to find someone recommended – otherwise you could be like a shop-owner client who came to me for advice, who had earlier been advised by an 'expert' on store layout. He closed for a week, spent thousands fitting out the shop to the submitted design – when the refit was complete, he didn't like it – and spent the next weekend taking it all out and restoring the original! Fitting out includes the outside layout/shape, appearance, signage, and display. Inside how will your displays be organised, what atmosphere, music (or not), image, merchandise groupings?

Don't forget too, the requirements of the Disability Discrimination Act, which requires all businesses (including small ones) to make reasonable changes to accommodate access to goods and services for disabled. This is not only about physical access.

13.4 Trading

'Retail is detail'. How many times has that been quoted? Yet it's in the detail that you will make your money – or lose it. The list of things to concern you is long and I can only address a few key issues.

The overall plan for your business will focus on your customers. It's not enough to say 'we sell xxxxx'. You are in business to meet customer needs – whether real and existing or new and created. Your sales 'package' or proposition will include the product range, the quality, the style, how it is displayed, store layout (which will include location as set out above). Someone once said that retail is about having 'right product, right quantity, right place, right time, right price, right appeal, and right service'. I'm sure you can add one or two more, but it's a good start point!

Earlier in the book, I have referred to the need to consider your customer base. Issues like age, sex, relevant fashion, social class and implications, could have radical effects on your business. How will you access/define customer needs, and then how will you meet them better than your competition?

Shop layout is a specialist area – for example, where to put the fast-moving stock, how to shift slow-moving items – and one area in which you may want expert help. At the very least, review all your competitors and see how they address such issues. You don't have to follow them, but at least you will be making positive decisions rather than falling into them.

Consider your stocking chain right from ordering to delivery. How much attention do you need to give to market trends, fashion, and technology? If you want to operate in a sector where you need to order your Christmas stock in February, you immediately have an idea of the timescales! Matters like credit terms are not just financial issues if part of your stock is goods on 'sale or return' from a keen supplier. Much of your wealth will be tied up in stock and therefore the establishment of your stocking policy deserves major consideration. Analyse how much you need to keep, of what types (and when you are up and running, keep track of what moves and what doesn't to improve your trading in the future). What about seasonality of sales – what is it and when do you stock up for it? How often does your stock turn over in a year (i.e. the annual cost of sales divided by the cost of stock)? How can you improve on this figure?

What are the margins in your business – and in the business chain? It's not uncommon for some businesses to need to mark goods up by over 100% (i.e. sale price is double purchase price) because of stockholding and operating costs. Can you cut out a link effectively? Find out what works and what doesn't as regards prices in the area – an expensive lighting shop is unlikely to do well in an industrial area – unless it operates as a discount 'shed'.

What will your policy be on breakages, on shop-lifting (a long word for theft), and customer returns – will you offer immediate refunds, credit notes, or nothing other than legal rights unless the goods are faulty? Perhaps the best advice is – decide on a range of policies such as buying on credit, 'lay-bys', returns and refunds, damage by customers, specials, sales, discounts etc. Deciding on a policy doesn't mean you can't change, but it gives you a standard.

Finally, on trading, plan your opening. See what assistance you can organise to get some media exposure (I've mentioned this earlier). You will be 'dead in the water' without your retail customers and you can't personally go out and drag them in – so how can you use the media to do so? Special opening offers? Invitations to local press reporters? Joint initial promotions with neighbouring non-competing stores?

13.5 Retail technology

Many believe that IT was invented to help the retail industry! Point of sale equipment enables you not only to collect cash and operate credit card payments, but also to keep detailed records of all your trading – what sells, when, in what quantities etc. You will need to make an investment initially, but it is likely to pay for itself in the short term by recording the vast detail of all the sales transactions and turning them into meaningful statistics to help you plan and manage the future of your business, by qualifying your decision making.

Whilst you may need expert assistance to specify the point-of-sale ('POS') equipment you will need, there is nothing to stop you doing a market survey of competitor shops to see what they operate. Probably the most important element of your IT system is the software you use – and the support you get after purchase from your software supplier. This is the manager and controller of your business, so spend enough time getting the right advice!

13.6 Key points

- There is a wide range of retail options. Try to 'bottom out' the best (for you) version of your ideas.

- Location is a very high priority in the retail industry and an expensive commitment. Research carefully before deciding where to go and signing a lease.

- You'll need to think through and plan the merchandising of your goods/services – down to very small details.

- Work from customer demands back through the supply chain, practically and financially, to understand how you will meet their needs.

- .

- .

- .

14

Business Services

14.1 Introduction

This chapter is for those people who really 'keep everyone else's wheels turning' – whether it's business-to-consumer or business-to-business. I have separated out consultancy (with its various forms) – which is one kind of service business – as this has some special requirements and is a major interest area on its own. Business services includes garages, estate agents, hairdressers, plumbers, carpenters, dentists, surgeons (and other dextrous skills), event organisers/performers and the events themselves, as well as nursing homes, hospitals, museums and employment/other agencies, hotels, sports clubs; in fact any business supplying intangibles. It's clearly a bit of a 'catch-all' category.

14.2 Customer satisfaction

In the area of service, there is no ongoing product for the customer to use from which to gain continued benefits – or to recall the purchase and from where it was bought. In fact it can be worse than that – your business could be servicing someone else's product which itself is unreliable and for which you may 'carry the can'. The key point to remember here is customer satisfaction. It may be that your business has repeat business – a car wash for example – or perhaps it's a once-off for most customers, e.g. real estate agency.

How many of us can recall that 'one time I had really good service' that we tell everyone about? But if I change the word 'good' for 'bad' or 'abysmal' in that sentence, we all have a tale to tell! It has been shown that, on average, we tell nine times as many people about poor service than we do about good service, so if service is your business, the first (and almost the only) thing to worry about is making (and keeping) customers happy.

So, listening to customers and making them feel exceptionally well looked after is where you want to be. Your customers should not want to stray to competitors, and you want them to recommend others to come to you. You also have to recognise that if you do not continue to provide exceptional service, there is little to stop them leaving you and going to a competitor. In this area more than most, it's not enough to be good at your job. You have to be seen to be much better than others. How you achieve this will depend on the sector and individual details of your business. It is the small details that make the difference – the dental surgery that rings you next day to 'see how you're feeling' after an extraction, or the garage that collects and washes the car every time it goes for service. Even if you charge more, it's providing the extra service that makes the difference.

Everything I've said earlier about knowing your service (and possibly products) and being able to define it, all aspects of research, marketing, and selling, apply as much (if not more so) to business services as elsewhere. The key issue is the service you give and living up to the 'promises' you give in your marketing literature, on the telephone, during sales presentations, and on delivery. You really do need to understand what your customers want and how you can over-deliver on it.

14.3   Providing the service

Let's divide this topic up into describing the service, delivery, and follow-up. In all three areas, customer-focus needs to shine through.

If you are providing a service on the customer's premises, most of the service description will take place in your marketing and advertising. Of special importance here is defining what you provide in terms that can be understood by the customers and meeting their needs. For example, a plumber may provide 'excellent plumbing and engineering services' or 'fix leaks and dripping taps quickly' – which would you ring first if you had a leaking tap? What would then happen when the customer rings; poor telephone manner can easily put off initial enquiries.

In delivering the service, it's possible for you to do a superb job – and alienate the customer at the same time. Some on-line providers of 'customer support' for computers or the internet seem to have the unhappy knack of pointing out clearly that it's because you are a moron that the PC/internet connection doesn't work – whereas others can tackle a similar issue with patience and good humour. As another example, if you promise to arrive – or deliver something on a particular day, you must do so. If you cannot, contact your customer first to advise of the delay and explain – and see if it is going to cause your customer a problem. If so, do something to 'rebalance' or recompense for the trouble.

On concluding the service provision, how much and how often do you communicate what has (and has not) been done for the customers – and does it demonstrate both your professional and technical expertise and skill, at the same time as your interest in the customers and their issues? Perhaps it isn't enough to say 'I've fixed it' and leave – maybe your customers needs more feedback.

Follow-up afterwards can be used to increase satisfaction and awareness – and to generate new business by securing the customer's loyalty. Perhaps a follow-up phone call, a personalised mailing, a focused customer survey? You should also consider how you can deal with complaints – accept them, and develop your business as a result. Listen carefully, understand the issue, acknowledge how the customer feels, and provide a practical resolution quickly.

14.4 Administration

The key feature of service businesses is usually the time spent on the customer's case. To avoid over- or under-charging, you will need to record and recover the time spent on each job, and for this you need some kind of time-recording system. This doesn't mean you will always invoice in full for the time booked – it may be your fault that the job takes longer than estimated/quoted. However, records of the time spent will help you avoid similar problems in future. Time recording systems may be manual or computerised and there may be relevant and useful industry specific packages you can purchase.

It may be viable for you to have a customer satisfaction return for completion after the end of the job. 'What could we do better?' is more likely to provide useful feedback and customer retention than 'Did we do the job well?' You want to be the best at what you do – as far as your customers are concerned – which is not necessarily the same as being the best in the country. It's about making your customers feel they are special to your business – and sometimes they are the best ones to tell you how!

Given that customer service is key, how you recruit and train your staff is also of paramount importance. They are your front-line troops in dealing with customers, and time spent on getting the right people, training them properly, and giving them appropriate discretion to satisfy the customer and deal with complaints can make a huge difference.

14.5 Key points

⎯ **'Services' is a big intangible – so you'll need to make a huge impression.**

⎯ **Focus all the time on being 'better than the best'. You want customers to return and recommend. Be the 'first choice, next time'.**

⎯ .

⎯ .

⎯ .

15

Planning Action and Staying Afloat

15.1 Introduction

If your background is from 'big business', one of the benefits you foresaw of setting up your own firm may have been the minimisation of paperwork – especially business plans! If you have never been in business before, maybe you don't see the need for, or even know 'how to prepare', business plans. This chapter is about the need for business planning – not as an end in itself, but as the propellant to get your business going in the right direction.

15.2 The business plan

Many people starting their 'own-business' do so in a services field which calls for minimal working capital but any business will require some funding, however small, and all will require a considerable investment of your time and energy. Finance may not be an immediate problem because you are seeking a second or support income, or because you have 'put by' enough in life savings, or that the business has limited financing requirements, or because you have received a severance payment from your previous employment. All these mean you can 'survive' for a significant period while income builds up.

Nevertheless, one central purpose of the new activity is to provide you with a 'satisfactory income' (however you personally define that phrase) and whatever you decide to do, there is the personal investment of time,

149

emotion, effort etc. I strongly recommend therefore that a Business Plan (defined here as a document outlining all the key aspects of your business and its strategy, not solely financial projections) is essential to achieve the objectives, whether or not there is a need to raise money either at the outset or after an initial period of trading. If you do not prepare a plan before you start, it is all too easy to delude yourself that your business is doing better than it really is. Before you set out on a journey, you do not need to know all the left and right turns, but you will need to know whether you are driving to Newcastle or flying to Rio de Janeiro!

You will need a business plan, to:

- consider the overall objectives and methods of achievement
- tabulate your thoughts clearly on paper so that you can later check them
- help your decision-making – is the investment of your time/money worth the risk?
- form a basis for you to raise money, if this is needed
- help you to monitor your business once it is launched.

A good place to start your plan is to spend some time considering your 'mission statement'. Much has been written and said over the years about these statements, some positive, some negative. However, the thought that can go into finding a few short phrases that define clearly why you intend to operate your business for the next few years can provide a clear focus for the development of a plan to do it.

Whilst there is no standard format for a business plan, the one outlined below is conventional and successful.

1) **Contents page** (for plans of over 10 pages).
2) **Summary:** a hard-hitting, succinct, enthusiastic summary of the whole plan. If this does not make a convincing case, no external investor will read further.
3) **Introduction:** outline, business objectives, purpose of preparing plan.
4) **Personnel:** details of key management and their expertise/experience; numbers and types of staff to be employed.
5) **Business history:** (if you are buying into, or diversifying, an existing

business) ownership, current products, markets, reasons for success, current financial position, recent financial history, why it is available for sale (if applicable).

6) **Product or service:** details and competitive edge you bring.

7) **Marketing:** market research, customers, marketing plan, suppliers and sub-contractors.

8) **Competition.**

9) **Premises and equipment:** details and costs.

10) **Legal aspects:** (such as licences, planning permission, patents, Health & Safety). Insurance (public, professional indemnity, employer's liability, loss of profit etc).

11) **Financial results/projections:** probably covering the first three years overall and with monthly details for first year. Cashflow forecasts, projected profit and loss accounts, balance sheets, pricing policies, key assumptions, assessment of risks and financial requirements, e.g. total investment, sources, timing, purposes, security offered.

If there is a wealth of **relevant** detail for any section, especially regarding the financial projections, you should include a summary in the plan itself and put all the details, together with full CVs of key management, in appendices.

The format of your plan may depend on the requirement of others, e.g. if you are receiving funding from a bank, they may require you to complete one of their standard packages. This may not be as comprehensive as the above format or may cover some aspects in more detail – you should prepare your own plans first – and may then need to develop other versions from it.

Key requirements of a good business plan are that it should:

● be succinct, professional and interesting – most plans are too long

● provide evidence of vision, market research, planning, financial control

● be convincing about the potential return on investment, the abilities of key management, show a clear understanding of customers and market, and show how a large and profitable market for the product/service offered will be secured.

Don't hesitate to obtain professional help in drawing up the plan, e.g. from your accountants, from Government agencies, or from corporate finance consultants for larger projects, or other specialists, but ensure that you write sufficient of it yourself for your enthusiasm to shine through.

Remember when you are submitting the plan for review by others, if they are not inspired by the summary, they are unlikely to read the plan – and if they do not read the plan, they will not meet you! Derive comfort from the fact that most plans are not written – they are rewritten, often many times! Test out your plan on others for their views. Further details of a Preliminary Business Plan are shown in Appendix II and those for a Full Business Plan suitable for presenting to institutional funders are shown in Appendix III.

15.3 The action plan

At some stage in the planning process, you must feel sufficiently confident that you have assessed the risks, maximised the opportunities, and minimised the threats sufficiently to launch the business. It will soon be time to launch – but not quite yet!

Check that you have thoroughly covered:

- **initial preparation:** self analysis, family consultation, the business idea, market research.
- **detailed planning:** outline business planning, investment needs, professional advisors, checks and precautions, legal steps, marketing and pricing strategy, full business plan.
- **setting up:** equipment investigations, systems & IT, stock estimates, funding requirements, financing, tax, premises, employees, marketing tactics and preparations.
- **launching:** final steps.

Review carefully your final steps to launch. Whatever the business, someone else may cause you to launch earlier than your plan, e.g. a customer wanting supply or a competitor who is first off the mark. Try to get in first to set out your own timescales for launch and stick to them.

Running a business nearly always requires acting on insufficient information – you will always be taking some chances because of this incomplete information. Success is more likely if you have thought through the options and alternatives, at least to some extent, and measured/planned for the risks. Some issues for you to consider now:

- when and how to launch
- initiating the marketing plan
- review of reference material.

It is good practice, however boring (!), to record and measure everything to learn what went well/badly, how you might have played it, where results came from, how long they took, how much resulted from what and so on.

15.4 Staying afloat

Once you are launched, how can you best make plans to keep your business on the right lines?

The key elements will be:

The required level of activity is the point at which an adequate income or profit can be expected, and one which is within the scope of money/capital employed in the business. In the first year, the required level may even show a loss, in order to establish the business soundly for the longer term.

Preparing realistic financial budgets that reflect the overall business plan. These must show:

- a monthly breakdown of sales/fees, costs, profit, and cash movement
- an annual overview of these items, showing how the longer term objectives of profitability and solvency are to be met.

Monitoring variances from budget is a vital monthly job, from which the next round of higher level business decisions can be made. To do this, it must be possible to extract quickly from your records a summary Profit &

Loss statement and Cash Flow after the end of each month. Your accountant will help you design a simple set of books and records for this purpose (Chapter 16). The cost of seeking a little more help at the initial stages is likely to be much less than the cost of the almost certain consequences of ignorance of the latest results when you are up-and-running.

Cash Control is essential in all areas of the business to achieve successful results. Here are four key areas:

- **Credit Control:** arranging settlement terms with your customers when contracting sales/fees so that payment may reasonably be expected on the due date; having a system to apply the most effective amount of pressure if payments are late.

- **Purchases:** planning to optimise order and delivery dates to obtain the best credit terms; settling bills regularly as a discipline, and not 'stringing out'. Making sure that the supplies coming in match the usage in sales going out. Planning just-in-time stocking/deliveries.

- **Overheads:** running a tight, well-planned business, perhaps leasing or renting equipment initially rather than outright purchase, or buying second-hand rather than new.

- **Capital Outlay:** looking very carefully at the pay-back periods before making commitments for major items.

15.5 Financially managing suppliers and customers

Even apparently successful businesses can fail through poor financial management of customers and suppliers. Issues range from payments made on-time, early, late, or not at all, to getting and giving fair deals.

15.5(a) Suppliers
Are you getting **good deals** from your suppliers? As well as price and delivery, what about financial terms? I'm not talking about taking advantage

of your suppliers and 'stringing out' your due payments well beyond the due dates. Some businesses have been launched by getting long-term supplier finance – where this has been in the supplier's interest.

I have talked earlier about the need for you to build relationships with your customers and the need for good relationships also exists with your suppliers – except it's your suppliers who need you and should be looking after you. Make it clear to them that you are looking for a **long-term relationship** when you are negotiating. Although you can go to a competitor, in general terms, neither you nor your supplier benefits if you do. Can you work with them on joint promotions? Is their quality and service up to par? Timescale of delivery okay?

Part of your supplier management is **stock control** – the importance of which varies widely depending on your business. Stocks (whether raw materials/purchases, stock in trade or work-in-progress, or finished goods) can account for a major part of the money tied up in the business. Managing your stock levels and purchasing on short timescales can make all the difference between success and hard times. It may even be better to pay more for your purchases to get faster-moving stock.

15.5(b) Customers

You will need to set up and implement **credit control** procedures to ensure that customers or clients pay you on time. Chasing money in is a vital task (and skill) which keeps your cashflow healthy – but it takes time, which is in short supply!

When starting with a new customer, it is normal to **seek trade references**, to understand what level of credit to give. These references can be from other suppliers and/or from credit reference agencies. Ask your customer for the trade references, but check the credit reference agencies yourself – it's not that expensive. Set out **your trading terms** clearly and, ideally get your customer to sign them. For your own use, set out your follow-up procedures to ensure that you are paid in accordance with your terms. Understand your customer's payment authorisation system – it is no use complaining about not being paid if the customer's buying department needs to authorise payment against an order number which you have not sought or supplied. Do you need to be registered as an 'authorised supplier'? Quote order and/or supplier numbers on the invoice, as well as the authorising manager. How are any queries on invoices handled by your customers? How often are cheque runs made? Follow up promptly as soon as any invoice becomes overdue. Keep a constant watch for any warning signs (if they are going broke, they won't pay you!). Keep notes of any conversations.

As well as credit checking new clients/customers, continue to do credit reference agency checks regularly, especially on large/key clients/customers. Don't run up big debts with customers about whom you know little!

Send out your **invoices promptly**, before the end of a month (some customers will take advantage if you invoice early in a month by paying at the end of the next following month). Be prepared to send out a statement at the end of each month showing what invoices are outstanding. If you have not been paid, write, telephone and if necessary visit to get paid. Visit the firm (if a regular client) and build up a relationship with a (named) person in the accounts section; if necessary talk to them daily if an invoice is outstanding. Make a note of what you are told and check to see if it is an excuse (e.g. the well-known 'the cheque is in the post'). You are now legally entitled to charge interest on overdue accounts (although you may wish commercially to talk to customers first before doing so); perhaps write informing them of your rights to do so and mentioning it clearly on your invoices. **Stop supply** if no payment is forthcoming. Seek partial payments. If necessary, consult your solicitor about taking legal action – it may not be 'being nice', but it's much more pleasant than going broke!

When times are tough, it's easy to let the basic disciplines go – 'there isn't enough time for all this admin!' But then you do not know where you are or what the priorities should be for you to do. Get a good book advising on credit control – such as *Implementing Successful Credit Control* by Alan Dixie, MB2000 – and implement sufficient procedures regularly enough to protect your business from others' incompetence or worse. Keep records of problems – it may be necessary to stop trading with certain customers or suppliers if their business practices are damaging your business.

15.6 Key points

- ⚷ Planning for success is essential. Set out briefly your objectives and how you intend to achieve them.

- ⚷ Refine your plans before launch.

- ⚷ Research, plan, do, hang in there!

- ⚷ Watch your cash.

- ⚷ .

- ⚷ .

- ⚷ .

16

Simple Records, Accounts and Book-keeping

16.1 Introduction

Your accountant will explain the books and records that must be kept to satisfy the law and I believe you should also discuss how to develop a simple system for you to produce monthly extracts measuring actual results against budget. The key point is that the records must be tailor-made for your particular business and should assist you in running the business.

Whatever the size of your business, the purpose of records and accounts should principally be:

(a) to help you manage and control the business
(b) to provide a written record of all transactions relating to the business
(c) to show whether you are making a profit or a loss and assist you to consider the cash flow implications (are you solvent?)
(d) to satisfy your bank, the shareholders, Revenue and Customs (tax and VAT) and to meet the legal requirements.

In addition, if you are operating a limited company, the maintenance of proper records and accounts is a requirement of the Companies Acts.

To achieve these purposes, it is essential that you keep the business records entirely separate from your personal records. In addition to setting up your own systems and procedures, you will certainly need to set up a business bank account. Any transactions of a personal nature that appear on the business account (e.g. personal drawings from the business or personal expenditure met by the business) should be recorded fully – for your own benefit and information – so that separation and analysis of business and personal items is easily done. Treat the business and yourself as if they are totally separate individuals, i.e. operating on an 'arms length' basis (as you would have done with any former employer). This applies whether you are operating as a sole trader or as a limited company. Open up a business current or cheque account for receiving and paying out money – and consider having a savings account for any funds you retain in the business for some time, e.g. for annual payments.

The complete process by which you record information and present it, i.e. book-keeping and accounting, is too complex to be addressed fully here. What is shown is a presentation of simple records and accounts suitable for a small business with a limited number of buying and selling transactions each month. A business this size would include a self-employed consultant or a business trading in a limited number of large items. Beyond this you will probably need a more complex form of accounting system. In any event you should seek the advice of your accountant in setting up and managing the system – who will be preparing accounts for you based on your records and the more time spent understanding the information you provide, the higher the accounting fees are likely to be.

It's worth noting here that there are many software packages available for smaller businesses which can do the job more than adequately. You will need to decide whether to start in business with one of these packages or whether to begin with a manual system. I start from the view that for a smaller business which will require only a few entries in the 'books', it's better to begin with a simple manual systems that you fully understand – but that if your business is more complex, you should start as soon as possible with the right accounting package. This chapter starts with the manual system – but refers to software packages. Whatever you do – you will need to understand what the system is doing! Remember too that the manual/paper based systems described are essentially the same as those operated by software systems – it's just that you have to complete all the bookwork for all the transactions by hand.

The examples shown also assume that you are registered for VAT; if this is not the case, make appropriate adjustments to the illustrations to omit the VAT elements.

If you are operating a retail business, some of this chapter will be of interest, but there are two main differences (a) you are likely to have a significantly greater number of transactions per month and (b) much of your business will be done on a cash basis. Talk through the details with your accountant and friends/colleagues in similar retail businesses and use those parts of this chapter and the Chapter 13 – Retailing as appropriate.

16.2 Operating the business

On supplying goods or services, you must submit suitable invoices promptly, which can be on a weekly, monthly or on an 'as required' basis. Invoices should be numbered sequentially and must be dated, with sufficient details of the services provided for the recipient company to recognise them and authorise the payment. The invoice should be addressed to the business concerned and should show the VAT amount separately. It must also show certain details about the business (there are different legal requirements for sole traders and companies), but always including the VAT number.

By and large, the greater the amount of detail, the more helpful and acceptable the invoice is to the recipient. Record the order number, person authorising the work, the dates the work/sales item was delivered/carried out, process, discounts, extras such as carriage/freight/expenses and your authorised supplier number (as relevant). Record too any special terms regarding payment, for example, payment within 7 days qualifies for a 5% discount.

I have shown sample invoices opposite for someone operating as a sole trader and another operating as a limited company which contain the required information. They are fairly self-explanatory, but note that the 'Tax point' is requirement in VAT legislation. This is the date at which VAT is payable, usually the earliest of the invoice date, the supply date, and the cash received date.

16.3 Sample Invoices

Self-employed example

BLUE MOON

6 Sunny Road, Thames Ditton, Surrey
Tel: +44 (0) 20 8458 0365   email: info@bluemoon.co.uk

INVOICE

Any Company Limited 30 Circus Mews Bristol BR1 2PW	Due for payment within 28 days of invoice date	Invoice No: 30502 Date: dd/month/yyyy Tax Point: dd/month/yyyy VAT No: UK 764 9556 81

To: Consultancy services in the month of September yyyy. *(you can then include details of the project work carried out).*

Or

To: The supply of XXXXXXX and XXXXX goods, including *(or excluding)* carriage and packing.

Plus expenses *or* carriage & packing

	Sub-total	
	VAT at **%	
TOTAL DUE		

Proprietor: Bob Self-employed

Limited company example:

BLUE MOON LIMITED

6 Sunny Road, Thames Ditton, Surrey
Tel: +44 (0) 20 8458 0365   email: info@bluemoon.co.uk

INVOICE

Any Company Limited 30 Circus Mews Bristol BR1 2PW	Due for payment within 28 days of invoice date	Invoice No: 30502 Date: dd/month/yyyy Tax Point: dd/month/yyyy VAT No: UK 764 9556 81

To: Consultancy services in the month of September yyyy. (*you can then include details of the project work carried out*).

Or

To: The supply of XXXXXXX and XXXXX goods, including (*or excluding*) carriage and packing.

Plus expenses *or* carriage & packing

Sub-total	
VAT at **%	
TOTAL DUE	

Registered in England number: ********
Registered office: 6 Sunny Road, Thames Ditton, Surrey

Keep copies of all unpaid invoices in date order in a separate file until they are paid. When payment is received, extract the invoice, noting the date of payment on it, together with the paying-in slip reference (or copy) and re-file in a 'paid invoices' file in cash receipt order. All payments received should be promptly paid into the bank, and you should enter the details into the Cash Book (see later).

For payments you make to suppliers, on receipt of the invoice from them, enter it into the Purchase Day Book (if kept, see later) and when you write out the cheque to pay it, write the date paid on the invoice together with the cheque number and enter up the details into the Cash Book. Keep the outstanding (unpaid) purchase invoices separate from the paid purchase invoices.

16.4 Records

The records described below are manual records, as these are all that are necessary and appropriate for a small business as described earlier; if you are operating a larger or more complex business, it may be worth investing in one of the sets of pre-printed accounting books (for manual records) or a well-known software package if you need to maintain your records on a computer. Obviously, there are computer systems that can cope with extremely large businesses; invest in a system of a size suitable for your needs; don't get a 'sledgehammer to crack a nut'. Don't automatically think that you need full or 'proper' double-entry book-keeping or computerised accounts for a small business; the time taken to enter and find data may be longer than if you prepared simple books manually.

There are many different ways of recording information – for every size of business. Choose the most appropriate. You may need to alter your system after you have set it up to meet the needs of your business, but with forethought (and help from your accountant, and a little luck!) you may get it right first time.

For the smaller business as described above, the records set out below will almost certainly suffice, the purpose being to record (in a manner simple and easy for you to use and keep up-to-date):

(a) the current cash position

(b) the business earnings e.g. sales or consultancy fees, with sales and VAT listed separately

(c) business expenditure, again listing the expenses and VAT separately, covering all the business expenditures, such as costs of supply, rent, rates, light, heat, phone, insurance, travel & subsistence, salaries of employees (but not your salary if you are a sole trader), NI contributions (company, not employee)

(d) trading amounts owed by you and to you at any time

(e) personal expenditure (you should record all expenditure).

To satisfy the requirements for a small business, you probably only need to keep a **Cash Book**; your accountant can probably keep any other records required, e.g. asset details. The cash book records all your income and expenditure with sufficient details to enable you to track the source document. An example of a simple cash book is shown on page 166. Where there are several small items such as phone calls from public call boxes, books, papers etc, you may wish to collate the costs in a **Petty Cash Book**, the totals of which are then transferred weekly/monthly to the cash book.

The cash book outline shown attached may either be drawn up by you on separate sheets of paper – it is then advisable to number the sheets (e.g. 'sheet 1 of 10') – or you can purchase pre-printed account books from a high street stationers.

For VAT purposes, you will need to keep information summarising and totalling your sales invoices showing the net amount, VAT and total amount and, separately, the same information for your purchases. In a large business, these would be called the **Sales Day Book** and the **Purchases Day Book**, but (as with the Cash Book) these may be kept on separate numbered sheets (see attached). You can also use these sheets to keep a close eye on the debtors outstanding (i.e. money owed to you) and the creditors (how much you owe) by reviewing the entries in the final column on each sheet. If you opt for the 'Cash Accounting' system for VAT, you may only need a Cash Book.

If your business is larger still with many transactions each week/month on credit with a range of customers and suppliers, you may also wish to keep details of your individual customers' and suppliers' accounts with you, i.e.

how much you have invoiced them for, the payments received with dates and the balance outstanding owing to you. You would need to draw up individual sheets for each customer similar to the sales day book example sheets. If you employ staff under PAYE terms, (including the case of your own company employing just you) you will also need to keep details of your payroll, i.e. the salary payments made to employees, together with the records required to meet the PAYE and National Insurance legal requirements.

You **must keep originals** of all source documents such as receipts for any payments you have made, petty cash slips for smaller items (with the receipts), bank statements, used cheque books and paying-in slips, together with copies of your (numbered) invoices. If you do not have a document, write out a note for the file giving details of this business expense. You **cannot recover the VAT** you spend when you purchase something if you do not have a VAT receipt, so get into the habit of asking 'May I have a VAT receipt please?' whenever you buy something (and keeping it)! A good way to file the documents is to have a lever arch file with separate sections for the cash book, sales invoices paid, sales invoices outstanding, purchase invoices paid, purchase invoices outstanding, VAT calculations, salary and PAYE. File the accounts summary sheet at the front of each section. Open a new file for each new accounting period/year.

For your own analysis and information, you may wish also to analyse the expenditure side of your cash book (traditionally the right hand side of the cash book), across a number of headings, e.g. raw materials, salaries and company NI, property expenses, subsistence and travelling expenses etc. This would involve setting up a number of additional columns to the right-hand side of the cash book payments sheet – or buying a suitable pre-printed analysis book. (And seek your accountant's advice.)

Try to enter up the information as it happens. It will be a lot more accurate and will take you less time than seeking to do it at the end of the month – or whenever – trying to remember if/when you paid that cheque out or finding the paying-in slip to record a receipt.

Treat money in your own business as you did/would have done in the business of an independent employer. Just because you are the owner of the business, you should not 'raid the till' if you need some cash. – which I imagine was precisely the case in your last employment!

16.5 Examples of records for a simple manual accounting system

Cash book

Receipts (Left-hand page)

Sheet xx of xx

Invoice Date	Invoice Number	Invoice Details	Net	VAT	Total	Date Paid

Enter the detail in the first four columns as it happens, totalling invoices received and banked in the fifth column when you make a payment into the bank.

Payments (Right-hand page)

Sheet xx of xx

Invoice received date	Supplier invoice number	Details	Net amount	VAT	Total	Date paid

Enter your payment as you write out the cheque, recording the date paid and the cheque number on the invoice – before filing it in the 'paid purchase invoices' file.

In addition, you may find it helpful to show details of all your payments by analysing the payments side (i.e. the right-hand side of the above) as follows (special analysis books can be purchased).

Cash book

Payments (Right-hand page)

Sheet xx of xx

Purchase Day Book	VAT	Travel Expenses	Telephone	Post & Stationery	Rent, Rates Service Charges	Utilities
Column 1	2	3	4	5	6	7

Utilities	Salaries & Wages	Drawings	Sundries			
Column 7	8	9	10	11	12	13

Column 1   is the total (net of VAT) from the Purchase Day Book

Column 2   is the VAT total due on columns 3 – 13 (equal to the VAT due on column 1)

Columns 3 – 13 should always be shown net of VAT

Sales Day Book

Sheet xx of xx

Invoice received date	Supplier invoice number	Details	Net amount	VAT	Total	Date paid

Purchases Day Book

Sheet xx of xx

Invoice received date	Supplier invoice number	Details	Net amount	VAT	Total	Date paid

16.6 Cash control

'Cash is King' is an expression used in banking and finance. Cash management – or the lack of it – is the key final reason for the success or failure of many businesses. It is ESSENTIAL that you keep a close control on your business cash to keep your business solvent and to avoid exceeding any arrangement you have with the bank for an overdraft – or going into overdraft if you have no such arrangement.

Insolvency is when a business cannot pay its creditors as they become due and to trade insolvently is an offence. If you do not have adequate records, you could find out too late that you have been trading insolvently – and the penalties are severe. If you ever get close to this point (and clearly we all hope you do not!) take early advice from a specialist and from your lawyer. For now, make every plan necessary to ensure that you never need to consider this situation in real life!

Cash is different from profit and your business can be profitable but have no cash, or (temporarily) be cash rich but unprofitable. If your business is selling goods profitably on credit, but not collecting its cash, you could be forced out of business. Alternatively, if you are selling goods at low margins or unprofitably but your customers are paying on time and your suppliers are granting you long credit terms, the end could be sudden!

Bank reconciliation

As part of your control procedure, you should regularly reconcile your cash book to the bank statements, adjusting for bank charges and interest, payments-in not yet received by the bank and cheques not yet presented, together with any standing orders and direct debits – and ensuring that the bank has made no mistakes. (Remember that it usually takes about four days for a payment into your account to reach it from another bank/branch, longer for a cheque you write and post to a supplier).

Start with your cash book. Add up all the receipts, take away the total of the payments and add the opening balance – giving you the closing balance/next month's opening balance. This cash book balance will probably not agree with your bank balance. Before going further, check the addition by totalling columns across and down.

Compare the cash book with the monthly bank statement and tick off the items that agree. Then adjust your cash book total with the uncleared cheques paid out and the payments in which have not reached the bank, to give you a revised total – which should then agree with the bank. If it does not, recheck your addition and perhaps pick up the entries you have missed until it does agree. When you have 'balanced the books', enter up in your cash book the missing items from your bank statement such as standing orders, direct debits, charges etc.

Check your unpaid customer invoices regularly to chase payment and to ensure getting paid. You may need to send out monthly statements summarising outstanding invoices, as some companies only pay against statements. Be prepared to chase payment by letter and telephone as necessary, politely and firmly. Although you are now entitled by law to charge a basic rate of interest on late payments, you may wish to consider introducing a clause into your terms of business allowing you to charge a higher rate of interest on such invoices which are outstanding; however, this requires the client's prior approval and may create an adverse impression. Check the supplier invoices you must pay to ensure the business can pay its way and you are still solvent.

16.7 Secretarial

Whichever format of business you choose (sole trader, partnership or limited company) there will be a certain amount of 'company secretarial' work to do – annual tax returns, correspondence with Revenue and Customs, the bank, and perhaps returns and forms to Companies House. The formal records for this can be maintained by you but may be better delegated to your accountant or other professional advisor. **Even so, the responsibility for the preparation, accuracy and submission on time remains with you.**

16.8 Key points

- Accounts and records are mainly to help you run your business. Make sure they do!

- You will have to meet legal and other requirements, but this should be simple if you have records adequate to run your business.

- Keep your personal money and records entirely separate from those of your business.

- Software isn't essential – sometimes basic manual systems are enough/better.

- Record information regularly and often – as it happens.

- Cash is the lifeblood of your business. Control its use.

- .

- .

- .

17

Summary and Conclusions

17.1 Introduction

Having reached this point, let us now make some assumptions.

- ☑ You have decided that you are the right sort of person or, at least, show sufficient of the necessary qualities and skills to start up the 'own-business' on which you have fixed.
- ☑ You have a clear idea for your 'own-business', you believe in it, and expect it to meet your income and retirement needs.
- ☑ You have discussed your plans with other sources of advice (as far as you can, without prejudice to your ideas).
- ☑ You have prepared a thorough Business Plan, which supports your decision to go ahead.
- ☑ You have engaged and used professional advisors.
- ☑ You will maintain an administrative system that provides a regular check on actual progress versus the plan.

Look for external advice and sources of help, but remember, you are in charge of timely decisions. Don't forget, too, the advertising slogan 'Ask the man who owns one'- talk to others running their 'own-businesses', similar to yours and dissimilar.

If you have completed all the above, you are clearly ready to get things under way and the sooner the better. TIME IS MONEY. So, now is the time to stop talking and start doing!

17.2 Some key issues to consider

Having read so far, you will have amassed a range of things to find out and do. If it seems insurmountable – remember that many do it, every week. Yes, you will need resilience to overcome the knocks, but knowing what could happen and how you might deal with it will help you face the difficulties.

● Are you wholly committed to running your 'own-business'? If not, it is essential that you continue to develop contacts and pursue all other suitable opportunities whilst you investigate fully the potential for your business. Should you take a full-time or part-time job until you have all the vital information?

● Have you – and the others concerned with/in your decision – the commitment, motivation, drive and are you (all) prepared for the risks? Persistence, perseverance, stamina and resilience are words often used by 'own-business' advisors! It's a long hard road, but it's worth it.

● Is your temperament suitable, are you entrepreneurial, can you take the hours, the time, the lack of holidays initially etc?

● Do your skills and interests relate to the business?

● Did your initial review of personal skills reveal suitable traits and skills for the current plan?

● Have you, or can you get, the necessary investment?

● Does your present review of skills and opportunities ahead suggest one form of business more suitable than others (retail shop or service business, consultancy, manufacturing, retailing, service, start-up or buy-in, franchising etc)?

● Have you set out a mission statement?

● Can you define the product/service, the market sector and the competition?

- Could you, should you, franchise?

- Have you done adequate market research?

- What is likely to happen to the market itself over the next 3 to 5 years? Can you stay ahead?

Remember that application and experience are needed – knowledge is not enough. Luck plays its part, but someone famous once said, *'Yes I'm lucky, but you know, the harder I work the luckier I get.'*

Possible additions to your action plan:

- Check with a public library or bookshop for available books and information on starting a business. Books are a very cheap form of training.

- Spend some time researching your idea, the competition (and all of) the market generally, small business, starting up etc. on the internet.

- Contact all local clearing banks for information packs on starting in business, franchising etc as appropriate.

- Talk to (local and central) Government agencies and independent organisations about training.

- Discuss plans with friends, family and other business people. Seek advice. **Don't ignore unwelcome advice.**

- Associate with other successful entrepreneurs and do similar things.

- Review your business plan and its detailed targets for achievement over the first 3, 6, 9, and 12 months. Are they realistic? Have you prepared fallback plans to go to another option if the first plans are not achieved? Success is not guaranteed!

- Analyse your experience and learn from it; apply developed methods, techniques, and learning in the future.

- Yes, I will say it – read and re-read this book, make notes, practise and develop your techniques and improve your knowledge. Each read should give you some new ideas, new applications.

GOOD LUCK – but more likely, MUCH HARD WORK!
You are the one who is going to make it happen.

Your own action points:

Appendix I
Further Reading

101 Ways to Succeed as an Independent Consultant, Timothy Foster, Kogan Page

Croner's Reference Book for the Self-Employed and Smaller Business, Daphne McAra, Croner Publications

Guide to Management Buy-Outs, Blackstone Franks, Economist Publications

High Income Consulting, Tom Lambert, Nicholas Brealey Publishing

How to Evaluate a Franchise, Martin Mendelssohn, Franchise World

How to Start and Run a Profitable Consulting Business, Douglas A Gray, Kogan Page

Leaflets published by each of the Clearing Banks on starting up in business, franchising etc

Lloyds TSB Small Business Guide, Sara Williams, Penguin Books

Pensions Simplified, Tony Granger, Management Books 2000

Private Company Secretary's Handbook, by Michael Harris and James Alexander, Management books 2000 (2006)

Starting a High Income Consultancy, James Essinger, Pitman Publishing

Successful Acquisition of Unquoted Companies, Barrie Fisher, Gower Publishing Group)

Taking Up a Franchise, Colin Barrow and Godfrey Golzen, Kogan Page

Taxation Simplified, edited by James Alexander, published annually by Management Books 2000

The Best Small Business Accounts Book, Peter Hingston, Hingston Publishing (www.hingston-publishing.co.uk)

The No-Nonsense Guide to Government rules and regulations for setting up your business, Business Link

Tolley's Tax Guide, published annually by Tolley Publishing Company

There is a wide range of books available on all aspects of setting up and running a business. None is a complete guide; the above list is a useful selection covering the major topics. Don't try to reinvent the wheel – if you read around, you may find a shorter way.

Visit your best local bookshop and browse through the 'small business' section. No one's book (even this one!) is going to provide all the answers. Which book to buy (first)? My advice is perhaps radical – check briefly through a few and the best one to buy will be the one you find most appealing to read! If it's full of fantastic detail but you find it impossible to pick up, it's pretty useless. I've read some poor business books in my time, but I have to say that every single one was able to contribute something.

Have a look too for reference books on specific business areas, for example, buying a post office, building and renovating houses for profit, running your own hotel, or whatever it is that you intend to do. It may not be a perfect guide, but someone has probably done it before you and you can profit from their experience.

Management Books 2000 has a good selection of books about starting and running businesses – visit their website at **www.mb2000.com** and seek out the section on Small Business.

Appendix II
Simple Financial Plans

Two sets of two sheets at the end of this appendix set out blank grids for a Profit and Loss Account and a Cash Flow. The first set assumes that your business is registered for VAT; the second set assumes it is not VAT registered.

For ease of use, you may wish to create these sheets for A3 paper, and print a number of copies for your use. They will need to be completed now with a plan and then on a month-by-month basis to compare forecast and actual results for the year – with similar sheets on a quarterly basis, say, for the next three years.

If you are fluent in the use of a spreadsheet such as Microsoft Excel, you will probably find it easier to set up a spreadsheet for the P&L and Cashflow using formulae to calculate the subtotal and total lines – but do ensure there are no addition or formulae mistakes! There are also specialist software packages and websites for business financial planning which may be useful – again depending on the complexity of your business and your own fluency with PC skills.

Completing the Profit & Loss ('P & L') account and cashflow

General

- In your first year, you will need to project results monthly; thereafter quarterly/annually is probably sufficient.

- Decide the units most appropriate for your business; two number accuracy will probably be sufficient.

- For each period, allow two columns – the forecast to be completed now, the actual as results occur.

- Make a note of any assumptions you make in developing the P & L and cashflow forecasts. You will need these to monitor results and you will need to provide such information to the bank if they require your forecasts.

P & L account

- In preparing the P & L account, exclude all VAT (unless you are not registered for VAT, in which case you must include VAT as a cost on all relevant expenditure items, but as you cannot charge VAT on sales, it will not appear in the sales section). This is because when VAT registered, all the VAT you pay out will be deductible from the VAT you charge on sales and which you collect on behalf of Revenue and Customs. The effect on your P & L for VAT registered businesses is therefore neutral. If you are not registered for VAT however, you will be unable to charge VAT to your customers and unable to recover the VAT you spend, so it becomes an added cost.

- Sales lines (A) – if necessary/appropriate, estimate sales by product group or type of business and then total. In projecting timescales, bear in mind the time taken to achieve sales from a cold start with a client.

- Direct costs – if you are supplying products requiring you to buy raw materials, put the estimated costs of manufacture in on these lines, allowing for manufacturing time. Do not include management salaries. For consultancy/services, this line will probably be blank.

- Overheads – if necessary, add to the sub-headings listed, but try to group costs in a way that will help you control them. 'Overheads' is basically the accounting word to cover all of those operating costs which cannot be directly related to products or services. Note that depreciation will usually not be the same as that used for tax purposes and should represent the cost of an item divided by its useful life; this will not necessarily 'put by' enough profit to purchase a new item, due to inflation, increased facilities etc. Bad debts can be terminal for a small business; no doubt you will take all precautions to reduce these to the minimum, but nevertheless you should include in your overheads a small percentage (2½% to 5%) of your turnover as a provision.

● Net profit – charge a salary (at an appropriate level) to the business for your own time, to see if you, as a shareholder, are entitled to dividends/drawings.

● You will need to complete the cashflow forecast to arrive at the projected overdraft in order to calculate the interest line on the P & L. This will again alter the cashflow etc. It is probably sensible to estimate generously the likely interest – and not iterate the calculations.

Cashflow

● In the P & L account, you include sales in the month that the sales are made and costs in the month they are incurred; in the cashflow the critical timing is when the cash is received or spent.

● In the cashflow, sales income (if you are registered for VAT) will be received with VAT. Whether registered for VAT or not, expenditure will be incurred with the relevant VAT. You will also make payments (probably monthly/quarterly) to the Revenue and Customs.

● The starting point for the cashflow is your opening business bank balance.

● In order to tie up with the P & L account, it may be easier to show the receipts from sales using comparable numbers and the receipts from VAT on sales as a separate line.

● You will need to estimate how much credit your customers will take, because even if you put 'net fourteen days' on the invoice, it is likely they will take considerably longer.

● Payments to suppliers – once established, you should be able to negotiate payment at the end of the month following the month of invoice – other than for cash items.

- PAYE/NIC payments to Revenue and Customs must be made by the 19th of the month following the month in which wages/salaries were paid.

- VAT (VAT on sales less VAT on eligible purchases) must be paid over at the due times. The standard payment is quarterly, which must be paid over by the end of the next following month. Monthly payment may be appropriate.

- Tax payments – do not forget to make provision for payment of corporation tax – or personal tax if operating on a sole trader basis.

- Rent/rates/water rates/telephone/heating/lighting etc – normally these bills arrive quarterly, which is how they will appear in the cashflow. You will probably find it easier for budgeting purposes if you spread these payments on a monthly basis when projecting your P & L.

- Capital expenditure – e.g. lease payments or car purchase should appear in the cashflow on the date of writing the cheque; they will appear in the P & L spread out over the months you are using them.

- Your opening balance, plus receipts minus payments, will give you a closing balance for the month – which then becomes the opening balance for the following month. You may find that the net result exceeds the bank borrowing facilities you have arranged – leading to a necessary revision to the figures.

- If you are not registered for VAT, there is no need to separate out VAT in the cashflow as no payments will be made to Revenue and Customs and no VAT is recoverable.

- In both the cashflow and the P & L, it is traditional to show negative items by enclosing them in ( )s.

Sample financial plan
Profit & Loss Account for [BUSINESS NAME]

All figures in £00 or £000 or £million

Months   Year total

PLAN/ACTUAL	P	A	P	A	P	A	P	A		P	A
Sales - category 1											
- category 2											
Total sales (A)											
Raw materials											
Direct labour											
Commissions/discounts											
TOTAL DIRECT COSTS (B)											
GROSS PROFIT (C = A – B)											
Salaries/wages/company NI											
Rent/rates/water etc											
Heat/light/power/phone											
Transport											
Packing/stationery/post											
HP/leasing											
Depreciation											
Professional fees											
Bad debts											
Advertising/promotion											
Bank interest & charges											
Other											
TOTAL OVERHEAD (D)											
NET PROFIT (C - D)											
Tax on profit											
Drawings and dividends											
RETAINED PROFIT(LOSS)											

Business registered for VAT – all figures are shown net of VAT

Sample financial plan
Cash Flow for [BUSINESS NAME]

All figures in £00 or £000 or £million

Months   Year total

PLAN/ACTUAL	P	A	P	A	P	A	P	A	P	A
Opening bank balance In credit/(overdrawn) (A)										
Cash from sales (received)										
Cash from debtors										
VAT on sales										
Other receipts										
TOTAL RECEIPTS (B)										
Payments to suppliers										
Cash purchases										
Salaries/wages/company NI										
VAT (net payments)										
Tax payments										
Rent/rates/water										
Heat/light/power/phone										
Transport										
Packaging/stationery/post										
Capital expenditure/HP/leasing										
Professional fees										
Advertising/Promotion										
Bank interest & charges										
Drawings/dividends										
TOTAL PAYMENTS (C)										
CLOSING BANK BAL. in credit/(overdrawn) A+B-C										
Cash introduced										
Closing balance carried fwd										
Agreed overdraft limit										

Business registered for VAT. All figures will include VAT in the cashflow, i.e. the cash that actually leaves the business, except that the sales are shown VAT-exclusive to agree with the figures shown in the P&L.

Sample financial plan
Profit & Loss Account for [BUSINESS NAME]

All figures in £00 or £000 or £million

Months   Year total

PLAN/ACTUAL	P	A	P	A	P	A	P	A	P	A
Sales - category 1										
- category 2										
Total sales (A)										
Raw materials										
Direct labour										
Commissions/discounts										
TOTAL DIRECT COSTS (B)										
GROSS PROFIT (C = A – B)										
Salaries/wages/comp'y NI										
Rent/rates/water etc										
Heat/light/power/phone										
Transport										
Packing/stationery/post										
HP/leasing										
Depreciation										
Professional fees										
Bad debts										
Advertising/promotion										
Bank interest & charges										
Other										
TOTAL OVERHEADS (D)										
NET PROFIT (C - D)										
Tax on profit										
Drawings and dividends										
RETAINED PROFIT(LOSS)										

Business not registered for VAT – all sales figures do not include VAT (it is not charged). All purchase figures include VAT

Sample financial plan
Cash Flow for [BUSINESS NAME]

All figures in £00 or £000 or £million

Months   Year total

PLAN/ACTUAL	P	A	P	A	P	A	P	A	P	A
Opening bank balance In credit/(overdrawn) (A)										
Cash from sales (received)										
Cash from debtors										
Other receipts										
TOTAL RECEIPTS (B)										
Payments to suppliers										
Cash purchases										
Salaries/wages/company NI										
Tax payments										
Rent/rates/water										
Heat/light/power/phone										
Transport										
Packaging/stationery/post										
Capital expenditure/HP/leasing										
Professional fees										
Advertising/Promotion										
Bank interest & charges										
Drawings/dividends										
TOTAL PAYMENTS (C)										
CLOSING BANK BAL. in credit/(overdrawn) A+B-C										
Cash introduced										
Closing balance carried forward										
Agreed overdraft limit										

Business not registered for VAT. All outgoings figures will include VAT in the cashflow, i.e. the cash that actually leaves the business. Income from trading has no VAT element.

Appendix III
Preliminary Business Plan

Introduction

One of the first documents you should prepare and review is a preliminary business plan similar to the outline attached. Some business ventures will need external financing and the provider of such finance will almost certainly require a business plan (both 'words' and 'numbers') as a precondition of involvement. Discussion and understanding of the plan will form a key part of the appraisal by the investment team of you and of the venture – before they look at the commercial returns. This discipline of convincing an objective investment business is absent where no such external funding is required, but even so, the resources (money and time) invested by you as the initiator of such a venture will be substantial. The preparation of a business plan will help you to assess the merits of your proposal and to consider whether or not to proceed along this route.

This plan outline has been prepared to help you in the initial appraisal of your ideas and will suit some business ideas better than others. If there are other factors critical to you or your business that are not referred to, please include them in the appropriate places. Consider each section and complete it as objectively and completely as you can, even if you have only a few facts, figures and hypotheses for certain parts. Sometimes looking at the gaps is as instructive as looking at the 'givens' in assessing whether the idea is worth pursuing or you personally have the determination to do so. Remember – writing down your ideas may help you to clarify them – and to try them out on friends.

When you have completed the document as far as you can, discuss it confidentially with a few friends, colleagues, contacts and other advisors.

If you decide to proceed with your business idea, this plan will lead on naturally to the preparation of a full business plan in due course – an example of which is shown in Appendix IV. You may find it useful at this stage (and will certainly later) to refer to one of the books on setting up in business, for assistance in any areas where you have difficulty. Sections of the plan that you are unable to complete will suggest further areas for personal research and for discussion with your friends, contacts and other advisors.

1. Summary

You may need to complete the rest of the plan before completing this page. Items 1.2 to 1.11 are 'one-liners', i.e. short, pithy statements, to summarise the ten sections on the following pages.

1.1   Description of business:

1.2   Objectives; long term goals:

1.3   Key management skills:

1.4   Review of the present business (if already existing):

1.5   The products/service, the market, the niche market and key competitors:

1.6   Why will I succeed? (Key competitive advantage)

1.7   How will I do it?

1.8   Main priorities for action:

1.9   Summary sales and profits:

1.10 Funding needed; from where?

1.11 Main expense items:

2. Objectives

2.1   My personal objective is (closest to):

(i) 'I already have (nearly) sufficient income; this venture is principally for personal interest.'

(ii) 'I need employment and to achieve material income to provide for my family. Be my own boss.'

(iii) 'I sincerely want to be rich and establish some serious capital.'

(iv) 'I want to be successful against my own criteria, but financial success is not critical. My definition of success is ....'

(v) (If none of these fits, please define your overall objective, mission here).

2.2   The business goals over the next 1/3/5 years are:

Year 1.

Year 3.

Year 5.

3. Management

You should prepare information 3.1 to 3.3 for each key member of management identified.

3.1   Name; CV/resume attached

3.2   Income requirements:

Year 1

Year 2

3.3   Key skills relevant to business:

3.4 Major management weaknesses relevant to the business and how to overcome these:

1.

2.

3.

4. Review of the present business

This section should only be completed if you have already started in business or have identified a possible target acquisition etc.

4.1 Audited accounts are attached:

4.2 Comments on growth to date:

4.3 Key strengths:

4.4 Major weaknesses:

4.5 Why is there an opportunity for change introduced by me?

4.6 Other:

5. The Market

5.1 What is the product or service offered?

5.2 What is the market?

5.3 Market size, potential, growth?

5.4 Are there different sectors?: (Product or Customer type), (International, national, local)

5.5   What's my niche or specialism?

5.6   Who are my customers? Retail, intermediary etc

5.7   Who are the competitors and what's their product or service? Ranking?

5.8   Thoughts on pricing?

5.9   How do I attract customers?

Marketing methods:

Selling methods:

Timescales to make sales:

5.10 Can I sell?

Experience?

5.11 Marketing strategy/plan:

5.12 Sales strategy/plan:

5.13 Operations plan:

How do I make it, buy it in etc.?

Employees:

Management information, controls etc:

6. Competitive advantage

6.1   What are customers actually buying?

6.2   Why will customers prefer to buy from my business? What's my competitive advantage?

6.3   Any evidence for this?

6.4   Competitor strengths/weaknesses?

6.5   How do I maintain my advantage?

7. How will I do it?

7.1   Are there options on how to get started in business?

7.2   If so, what are the merits/drawbacks of each?

7.3   Comparative risks of each:

7.4   Preferred option and why:

8. Main priorities for action

I intend to start my business on: dd/mm/yyyy

8.1   What are my immediate needs for action?

8.2   Premises:

8.3   Equipment needs:

8.4   Orders/contracts in hand?

8.5   What if it ...

-    **Grows faster?**

-    **Grows slower?**

-    **Other?**

-

9. Sales and profits

It would be helpful to complete as much of the financial schedules 1 and 2 as possible to give an idea of the results to expect and the financing required. At this stage, do not seek to be too accurate.

9.1   Key assumptions used in preparing financial schedules:

9.2   Non-financial targets:

10. Funding needs

The financial projections in the appendices may show some funding requirements. How are these to be met?

10.1   My own investment:

10.2   My security available to lenders:

10.3   Other investor(s) and their stake(s). How they will invest:

10.4   Thoughts on debt or equity investment by others:

-    amount:

-    type (hire purchase, loan, overdraft, factoring, equity investment/ shareholding etc):

- the percentage equity I would release:

10.5 Thoughts on structure (limited company, sole trader, partnership, other) and why:

10.6 Grants I have identified?

11. Key expense items

What are the major items of expense in setting up your business (e.g. property, equipment, marketing/advertising, stock etc?).

	Item	Cost	Comment
11.1			
11.2			
11.3			

SCHEDULES to the preliminary business plan

The preliminary business plan requires, for completeness, some financial information. I set out earlier (pages 183-186) some outlines for a Profit and Loss Account and Cash Flow statement, together with brief guidance on completion. You should aim to have month-by-month information for the first year, and then year-by-year plans, for each of these, against which you can monitor the actual results.

Writing and Using a Full Business Plan

1. Introduction

Good planning is accepted as being of prime importance among successful companies, large and small; it can, however, be seen as an unnecessary chore by those starting out in business or planning the purchase of an existing business.

The purpose of this appendix is to explain the importance of planning, based on the type of business plan that institutional investors would like to see and on the financial institution assessment process. It is not intended to set rigid requirements, but rather to guide and suggest an approach that will help you to assess your project wisely. If you do not require institutional funding, it does not remove the need for a plan. You will be investing your time, and the cash investment you make into your business will possibly be the second or third largest cash investment you will ever make.

You should be as tough and professional in your assessment of the advisability of the investment as any professional investor. The writing of a well-thought out and researched business plan is a challenge in itself and should help you in the appraisal of the business opportunity. Without a plan you have no yardstick by which to measure whether you are making progress towards your objectives – or not.

2. Why is a plan important?

Leaders of organisations have always planned and the efficiency, survival, and growth of a business testify to the quality of the planning its leaders have done. Some planning is done formally, but a good deal more is done instinctively. However, the increasing size and complexity of businesses and the rapid changes in the commercial environment require an increasingly formal approach in assembling and analysing information.

In seeking an equity partner, the importance of reaching an agreed philosophy on the way forward cannot be over-emphasised, as the company and its new investor will be working together for a number of years. The partners should therefore be agreed on the main objectives, the way these should be achieved, the methods of monitoring, and how any necessary changes can be implemented.

Planning is not an end in itself, it is an action-orientated process. We can only influence our future by the actions we take today, and planning helps us to ensure that today's actions will help us towards tomorrow's objectives. Planning is an entrepreneurial activity calling for creative thinking. It cannot be completely accurate because basic assumptions are always changing; the plan must deal with probabilities and trends. As such, it is the rationale that lies behind the selection of strategies and the tactics to achieve the goal that are more important than any detailed figures.

Good plans are concise and record only the relevant facts and reasoning to describe the proposed actions and their necessary implications. Excessive detail, especially in the plan 'numbers', distracts attention from the essential strategic features and suggests a degree of accuracy that may be misleading. It is much more difficult to write a short plan than a long one – Voltaire is reported to have said:

> *'Madam, here is the novel you commissioned. I am sorry it is in two volumes – had I had time, I would have written it in one.'*

A short plan is much more likely to be understood and to give a sense of direction.

If you are going into business with a partner, it is critical that you understand each other's goals, motivations, strengths and weaknesses etc. The preparation of a comprehensive business plan will assist greatly in this.

3. Business plans and investors

If you seek outside investment, a business plan will be an essential requirement during the investor's initial appraisal. It is likely to be `bound into' the investment agreement at the end of the negotiations, and the discussion and agreement of the plan will help you to share goals and understand objectives.

Investors do not seek to agree a firm detailed plan to cover the next five years; rather they look to achieve common thinking on objectives, review procedures and action programmes. As the business environment is constantly changing, investors will seek to review plans and objectives at least annually.

To some extent your business plan is a selling document and if it is not attractive, it will not be read! Your presentation must be positive and realistically enthusiastic. The key requirement remains (for most investors and especially for you) that it should be a good reference document for the business.

Remember – a venture or development capital institution is not appraising whether to make an investment in your business, whether the plan is sound, or whether the returns are adequate. Not at all! The investment executive will have to convince the review committee that the plan is the one chosen out of the one or two hundred seen, which represents a better return (at acceptable risk) than leaving the cash where it is presently invested – and that the cash will remain better invested in your business until such time as the investment can be unlocked. The investor's assessment of this timing is likely to be later than yours.

The three key criteria that an investor seeks in the decision-making process have been humorously described as: management, management and management. This emphasises that the assessment of management (qualifications, experience, track records etc) comes well before assessing markets, product/services, USPs etc.

4. The planning process

Ideally, there are a number of stages in establishing a business plan, which may be as follows:-

(i) Establishment of the medium/longer term objectives of the business and the basic policies within which it will operate.

(ii) A careful analysis of the past/present performance of the business (if it already exists), the environment within which it exists (or is to exist) and the outlook for the future. Special note should be taken of constraints that are likely to limit the freedom to adopt strategies (e.g. cash, manpower, and management) and the opportunities perceived.

(iii) The evaluation and selection of strategies that are the best among the available alternatives to enable the business to meet its longer term objectives.

(iv) The specification of the targets to be achieved in order to effect the chosen strategies, which will lead through to budgets and individual operating targets.

(v) The preparation of the 'numbers' – essentially a product of the strategic thinking and action programmes planned.

5. The business plan profile

While each business will (and should) produce a business plan in its own format, the following represents one plan layout comprising eleven sections plus appendices that may be appropriate.

5.1 Summary – A hard hitting, succinct summary of the following 10 sections, which omits all the unimportant detail. If this section does not make a convincing case, no external investor will read further. Even if you are not seeking external investors, the preparation of this section will help you (and your family) to decide whether the investment – time and cash – is likely to be worthwhile.

Key points: the business and its competitive advantage, key achievements, people, profits – past and future (and potential return to investors if relevant). One to two pages, maximum.

5.2 The main business objectives and policies, the `mission statement', which should be quantified and timescales for achievement given. It is probably appropriate also to establish any limitations to the business e.g. geographic or technological, imposed or chosen.

5.3 The management team – their track records/experience, remuneration, equity in the business and other commitments (if any). Management team strengths and weaknesses.

5.4 Review of progress of the existing business (if any) over the last three to five years in financial and non-financial terms. Refer to any previous plans and explain major variances.

5.5 An appraisal of the business environment: the market size and growth, competition, technology advances, market shares etc. Home and overseas. Sectoral analysis. Customers and customer analysis.

5.6 An objective appraisal of the products and services and the business – its/their strengths and weaknesses, and the threats and opportunities facing it/them. The competitive advantage vis-à-vis the competition.

5.7 An overview of the main strategies available in establishing or growing the business, the comparative risks and benefits of each and the main elements of the chosen 'best option'. The subsidiary strategies (e.g. marketing, production etc) covering especially how competitive advantage will be maintained, i.e. maintaining the 'edge'.

5.8 The action plan – detailing out the key objectives (e.g. new products, sales and marketing, manufacturing, personnel etc), priorities and actions required to achieve the main elements of the Plan. How to market and sell the product/service.

5.9 Performance targets – the results expected and by which achievement of the plan will be measured. The targets will include those of a financial nature (e.g., sales, profit & loss and balance sheet details), numerical ones (e.g., product volumes, market shares etc) and other milestones such as new product introductions. Two-figure accuracy is usually sufficient. List key assumptions and sensitivities.

5.10 How the business is to be funded: covering internal cash generation, external cash available, additional funding required from shareholders and/or new funding sources.

5.11 Principal opportunities that could emerge and risks that could be met in this plan and contingency plans for reducing these risks.
- 'What if' assessments, i.e. altering a few key variables and seeing what happens.
- For existing businesses, details of any significant changes in strategy from previous plans, with reasons for the changes.

5.12 Appendices should be attached (or be available) including key assumptions, the plan data – detailed profit & loss accounts, balance sheets, cash flow statements, key ratios, capital spend, product line analysis etc. For existing businesses, these must include the last three years audited accounts, with any major variations fully explained.

6. The investment proposal

If you are seeking external finance, then, in addition to the normal business plan, investors will require certain other information, which will to some extent depend on the individual business.

As a rule, they would certainly need:

- Full CVs on the founding management, i.e. the people who will make it happen. Professional references will also be needed.
- Any uniqueness in, and the associated protection of, the company's products.
- Details of proposed investment required and the risks perceived.
- More extensive 'what if?' analyses and contingency planning.
- Plans for the eventual realisation of the investment, i.e. the investor's exit.
- Most recent audited accounts, details of banking arrangements, mortgages etc.
- Current order book and key customers.

Since different investors may have differing criteria for investment (returns, exit routes, debt/equity ratios and forms of investment), you should make some simple assumptions for these, but create financial models that will allow you to re-run the numbers as required.

7. Conclusion

The business plan and the investment proposal are essentially means to achieve an end, namely the profitable, substantial growth of the company. The plan should concentrate on relevant major issues and should be prepared principally to be of use to the business, although when external investors are likely to be involved, clearly some background will need to be given for the information of your potential new equity partner.

8. Presentation

First of all, **content**. Being involved in the detailed analysis can lead professional managers to overlook fundamentals. One of the most common misconceptions is to prepare the plan from the single viewpoint of the owner, inventor or entrepreneur, i.e. usually the writer of the plan. Good plans are written by balancing three different perspectives – those of the entrepreneur, the investor and the market/customers. Marketing from the customers' point of view is probably the key issue for investors after the appraisal of the management and these two are usually the keys to success. In this context, the word 'investors' also includes the founder(s) who have to decide whether the investment will be worth the time and money they are investing; a job may be a better option.

Financial results are NOT the business plan. Masses of spreadsheets will not disguise an ill-considered strategy or poor appraisal of the market. Plans with inches of spreadsheet number-crunching are much less likely to be read than concise, well-written plans including summary numbers for three years' projections – with further details available if and when required.

Packaging – appearance is important, but a word-processed document in a spiral bound booklet with stiff card covers is fine – you do not need the plan to be specially printed in colour, properly bound, with pie-charts etc.

Length should be no more than about 12 to 15 pages plus appendices, with the general guidance that the more money required for investment, the longer the plan is likely to be (Section 10 gives more detailed guidance on length). Edit your first draft – and then edit it again! Remember to include your name, address and phone/fax, to number the copies and, especially if sending the plan out to institutional investors, ask for the plan to be returned if they do not wish to pursue the possibility of investment.

9. Advice

You may wish to seek some professional assistance in preparing the plan, depending on the complexity of your business and on whether you are seeking external/institutional investment. Consider the pros and cons of this course carefully, together with the track record of the advisor, and discuss this with people whose opinions you value. Assistance is available from accounting firms (the larger ones will have specialists), from corporate finance 'boutiques' and other small specialists, from business colleagues and from some Government agencies.

Whatever advice you take, preparation of the plan is the CEO's responsibility – do not get someone else to write the whole of your plan.

10. The business plan in detail

This proposal of a detailed format for a business plan should be amended as appropriate for your business. The starting point for preparation should be the Preliminary Business Plan shown in Appendix III, your subsequent market research, and analysis among your contacts, your reading of (one of) the many books on the subject and/or from one (or more) of the excellent publications available from the banks or accounting firms. You could also look at publishers of software for business plans – such as Palo Alto Software (**www.palo-alto.com**).

The cover of the plan should show your/the company's name, address and phone number, the plan title, number and date, and any disclaimer you wish to make, together with a statement that the plan is confidential. The page inside the cover should be a detailed 'Contents' page.

10.1 The summary (One/two pages)

The summary is really a plan within a plan, being complete within itself. In a convincing, concise narrative form, you should explain the nature of the business, the market and the products, the business potential and its competitive edge.

Be realistic, brief, but enthusiastic!

Key topics (select from, as appropriate):
- Name of company; location; stage of development.
- In what business(es)? In what market segment(s)?
- Products, present and potential.
- Summary track records of key managers.
- Names and affiliations of directors.
- Competitive advantages, product differentiation, proprietary technology.
- Size and growth rate of the company's domestic market segment(s).
- Domestic competition (direct and indirect).
- Size and growth rate of company's international market segment(s).
- International competition (direct and indirect).
- Management's goal for the enterprise. Timetable.
- Strategy and tactics for attaining that goal.
- Principal risks and contingency plans.
- Projected market shares, domestic and international.
- Financial performance to date (in short form to two-figure accuracy).
- Financial projections, including cash flows (short form).
- Investment proposal; funding sought. For what percentage ownership?
- Timetable? Uses of funds?
- Investors' exit route and returns.

10.2 Business objectives/policies (One page)

- What is the business to be?
- What is the mission or business goal?
- How long will it take to get there?
- In what market sector and geographic area does it/will it operate?
- Any restrictions, imposed or chosen on the growth of the business – these could be technology issues, commercial issues or factors chosen by management.

10.3 The management team (One page plus appendix)

Include a general description of management and their shareholding in the body of the plan, with detailed CVs/resumes in the appendices. The plan should comment on how long the team has worked together, what distinguishes them and any major achievements.

In the appendices, the CVs could be developed to show specific experience relevant to the business venture. Do not feel you have to put in CVs for every member of the management team but you would certainly need to include all the key investors. If you are predicting rapid growth, it may be appropriate to show how the management structure will develop; this is not normally required.

10.4 Review of the business (One page plus appendix)

Where the plan is being put together to consider the acquisition of an existing business, some appraisal is required of where that business is now and where it has come from.

Key topics:
- When the business was started.
- A summary of how it has progressed and present stage of development.
- Highlight any past successes.

- Key financial results, including the last three years sales and profits and any particular 'humps and hollows' and the causes for the same.
- Present management.
- Shareholders.
- If you are proposing a new departure for the business, how this has arisen. If the business has been unsuccessful in the past, how are you going to make a significant difference – in order to change the 'habits of a lifetime' of the business?
- Audited accounts should be available, but only include P&L, balance sheet and cashflow pages, unless there are other important items – e.g. auditors' qualification of the accounts.
- Any particular market position company has built – and how.

10.5 The business environment (Two/four pages plus appendix)

This section needs to provide a comprehensive overview of the market generally, the customers, and the competition.

For the market generally, assess the overall size, past growth rates and future prospects, how the market is segmented into particular niches – identify the company area, technology trends (or other issues) affecting the market as a whole and/or the company niche, prospects for the company specialisation, the domestic/international market. Any independent data?

In reviewing the customers you should consider whether they can be segmented, whether there are different buying patterns, who makes the decision to buy, who has the purchasing power in this sector, customer type, industrial or consumer, order sizes.

Competitors should as far as possible be identified, with comment on their size, potential, technology etc, what market share they enjoy; what their strengths and weaknesses are; how profitable, reputable, stable etc; how you can compete with them successfully and their likely response to your market entry/change. What you can control – and what you cannot control.

In reviewing marketing generally, what are the traditional lessons of marketing in this country, overseas, what is pricing policy, the position on after sales service etc? Detailed appraisal would be in the relevant appendix.

10.6 Appraisal of the product/services and of the business (One/two pages plus appendix)

Depending on the nature of the business, this may be one section or two. Often, with a product-based company, the strength of the business is intricately linked with its products; in other cases, it may be more sensible to have one section dealing with the products/services and their particular strengths/weaknesses and then as a separate section the overall business and its strengths/weaknesses.

What is the product/service, what does it do?
- Why is it different?
- What are the competitive products/services; competing technologies?
- How will the product development go?
- Protection (patents, trademarks).
- Costs/margins.
- Any disadvantages, short term problems etc.
- Barriers to entry v. competition.
- Lead times, life cycle.
- New product development.
- National approvals required. Industry standards.

In reviewing the complete business, you should highlight the SWOTs (strengths, weaknesses, opportunities and threats). In analysing the strengths, it should be clear that you are building on these to expand and develop the business and in reviewing the weaknesses, considering how to overcome/rebuild/replace. The opportunities ahead should be identified and it should be clear how these will be addressed and your actions for dealing with the threats facing the business (from outside intervention).

You will have considered earlier the competition and it is worth considering here what the competitive advantage is and how it will be maintained/improved.

For a manufacturing company, it may be appropriate to include a section on the manufacturing technology and its development, production facilities and employees.

Again, relevant but detailed comments could be assigned to the appendix.

10.7 The business strategy (One page)

In reviewing your plan, the investor will want to be sure that you have considered other strategies and/or strategic options for taking the company forward, and sufficient detail about these should be included to show that you have considered them thoroughly. Each option will have its own risks and benefits and you will have been through a reasoning process, which should be included, if necessary as an appendix, to state why you have chosen the course you have. In detailing the subsidiary strategies, e.g. for marketing and production, you should not go into reams of detail and risk boring the reader, but rather present the essential information in a way that is straightforward to understand.

10.8 The action plan (One/two pages plus appendix)

The whole purpose of the business plan is to lead through to action. State the key action points in the plan, but again, not in masses of detail. By all means have subsidiary detailed plans available, should an interested investor want to follow up (and for your own use), but these may need to be reviewed regularly and should therefore be separate documents.

10.9 The performance targets (Two pages plus appendix)

The body of the plan will contain summary information on the key milestones for the next three years, year total P&Ls, cash flows, overall market shares etc; detailed information, including the full P&L, balance sheet and cashflow, first year by month, should be consigned to an appendix. Similarly, key assumptions should be in the main plan with a larger list as the preface of the appendix.

Financial results should be presented to two-figure accuracy. An analysis of sensitivities to prices, costs, volumes (including effects of slippages of six and twelve months in sales-growth projections) should also be presented.

I have included an outline for the P&L and Cash Flow in Appendix II, for operating the business. The details required here are the same for the P&L,

but the cash flow is extended to consider the introduction of long term cash. Attached is a summary of the P&L, Cash Flow and Balance Sheet. Include summarised figures in the plan, with detailed figures in the appendices.

10.10 Funding (Less than one page)

Refer to any past external funding, the future need and how it will be met.

10.11 Appendices

You will note from the above that appendices may be needed for

- Management CVs (Section 10.3)
- Audited Accounts (Section 10.4)
- Market Information (Section 10.5)
- Product/Service information, brochures (Section 10.6)
- Detailed action plan (Section 10.8)
- Performance Targets, Profit & Loss Accounts, Balance Sheets, Cashflow projections etc (Section 10.9)

You may also want to include details of professional advisors (bankers, accountants, lawyers). Consider whether to bind these appendices into the plan – or have them available as a second volume.

Profit & Loss Account

	Plan	Actual	Plan	Actual
	Year by year in plan, monthly in appendices			
Sales				
Cost of goods/services				
Indirect overheads				
Profit before tax				
Profit after tax				

Balance sheet

	Plan	Actual	Plan	Actual
	Year by year in plan, monthly in appendices			
Fixed assets (tangible/intangible)				
Stock				
Debtors				
Cash				
Creditors				
Loan stock				
Net assets				
Share capital				
Share premium				
Retained P&L				
Shareholders funds				

Cash flow

	Plan	Actual	Plan	Actual
	Year by year in plan, monthly in appendices			

Cash flow from operations

   Sources

      Sales

      Other income

   Less Uses

      Cost of goods

      Indirect overheads

      Investment in fixed assets

   Cash flow from operations

Non-operational cash flow

   Sources

      Equity increases

      Loan increases

      Sales of investments

   Less uses

      Loan repayments

      Interest

      Taxation

      Dividends

Net cash flow

Projections in the appendix should be monthly for year one, then annual results only. Don't go to extremes with the numbers; they must be realistic and achievable – if stretching.

Appendix V

Sources of Funding

The most commonly used institutional sources of funds for new businesses are the clearing and merchant banks. Leasing and factoring companies, including those who are part of the clearing banks, are likely to provide money which is more expensive but can be very valuable for early-stage businesses. Specialist finance, such as business angels, venture and development capital firms, provide a significant volume of business finance, but are more likely to be involved in providing larger sums for second round or business development finance. Typically, venture/development capital organisations will not invest less than £1 million and are not at all keen on start-up ventures.

The following organisations can provide advice and assistance:

British Venture Capital Association, 3 Clements Inn, London WC2A 2AZ
tel: 020 7025 2950 **www.bvca.co.uk**
(for a list of venture capital and business angel sources)

3i Plc. Offices in many parts of the UK and internationally, principal UK ones being: 91 Waterloo Road, London SE1 8XP, tel: 020 7928 3131, **www.3i.com** and 227 West George Street, Glasgow G2 2ND tel: 0141 248 4456

Scottish Enterprise, 5 Atlantic Quays, 150 Broomielaw, Glasgow G2 8LU
tel: 0141 248 2700 **www.scottish-enterprise.com**
(for details of Scottish support)

Companies assisting those seeking funds to get in touch with potential private investors include:

VCR Limited, 7 Old Park Lane, London W1K 1QR tel: 020 7629 9949
www.picapital.co.uk
(publishers of Venture Capital Report)

The National Business Angels Network, tel: 020 7329 2929
www.bestmatch.co.uk

Appendix VI
Useful Addresses

Advisory Conciliation and Arbitration Service (ACAS)
Brandon House, 180 Borough High Street, London SE1 1LW, Tel: 08457 474 747
www.acas.org.uk

Association of British Chambers of Commerce
1st Floor 65 Petty France, London SW1H 9EU, Tel: 020 7654 5800
www.chamberonline.co.uk   or **info@britishchambers.org.uk**

Association of Corporate & Certified Accountants
64 Finnieston Street, Glasgow G3 8DT, Tel: 0141 582 2000 **www.accaglobal.com**

British Franchising Association (BFA)
Franchise Chambers, Thames View, Newtown Road, Henley on Thames Oxon RG9
1HG Tel: 01491 578050 **www.britishfranchise.org.uk**

British Insurance & Investment Brokers Association
(For local brokers or quotes on e.g. Professional Indemnity Insurance)
BIIBA House, 14 Bevis Marks, London EC3A 7NT Tel: 020 7623 9043
www.biba.org.uk

British Technology Group (Technology licensing etc)
10 Fleet Place, Limeburner Lane, London EC4M 7SB Tel: 020 7575 0000
www.btgplc.com

Business in the Community
137 Shepherdess Walk, London N1 7RQ Tel: 0870 600 2482 **www.bitc.org.uk**

Business Link
Tel: 0845 600 9006 **www.businesslink.org**

Central Office of Information
Hercules Road, London SE1 7DU Tel: 020 7928 2345 **www.coi.gov.uk**

Chantrey Vellacott DFK (accountants)
Fao E Harris Partner, Derngate Mews, Derngate, Northampton NN1 1UA
Tel: 01604 639257 **www.cvdfk.com**

Chartered Institute of Management Accountants
26 Chapter Street, London SW1P 4NP Tel: 020 7663 5441 **www.cimaglobal.com**

Chartered Institute of Marketing,
Moor Hal, Cookham, Maidenhead, Berkshire SL6 9QH Tel: 01628 427500
www.cim.co.uk

The Chartered Institute of Patent Agents
95 Chancery Lane, London WC2A 1PT Tel: 020 7405 9450 **www.cipa.org.uk**

Companies Registration Office
Companies House, Crown Way, Maindy Cardiff CF4 3UZ Tel: 0870 333 3636
www.companieshouse.gov.uk

Competex Ltd (business accounting for consultants)
Orchard House, Park Lane, Reigate, Surrey RH2 8JX Tel: 01737 234567
www.competex.co.uk

The Countryside Agency
John Dower House, Crescent Place, Cheltenham, Gloucester GL50 3RA
Tel: 01242 521 381 **www.countryside.gov.uk**

Department for Work & Pensions
Correspondence Unit, 1-11 John Adam Street London WC2N 6HT
Tel: 020 7712 2171 **www.dwp.gov.uk**

Department for Work & Pensions (for new employers) Tel: 08456 070 143
www.dwp.gov.uk

Department of Trade and Industry (DTI)
Enquiry Unit 1, Victoria Street, London SW1H 0ET Tel: 020 7215 6740
www.dti.gov.uk For Business Link, tel: 0845 6009 6006 – **www.businesslink.org**

Design Council
28 Haymarket, London SW1Y 4SU **www.design-council.org.uk**

Environment Agency
Tel: 0845 933 3111 **www.environment-agency.gov.uk**

Franchise Development Services Ltd
Franchise House, 56 Surrey Street, Norwich NR1 3FD Tel: 01603 620301
www.franchise-group.com   info@fdsltd.com
(Commercial Advice re Franchising – internationally)

Health & Safety Executive
HSE Infoline, Caerphilly Business Park, Caerphilly CF83 3GG Tel: 08701 545 500
www.hse.gov.uk

HM Revenue and Customs Department
Tel: 08459 154515 (Tax) 0845 010 9000 (VAT) **www.hmrc.gov.uk**

Independent Financial Advisor
Smart & Cook Financial Services, 4-6 Ripon Road, Harrogate, HG1 2HH
Tel: 01423 700745 **www.smartandcook.co.uk**

Information Commissioner
Wycliffe House, Water Lane, Wilmslow, Cheshire SK9 5AF
www.dataprotection.gov.uk

Inland Revenue (Now merged with Customs and Excise to become HM Revenue
and Customs Department)
Tel: 08459 154515 **www.inlandrevenue.gov.uk**

Institute of Chartered Accountants of England and Wales
PO Box 433, Moorgate Place, London EC2P 2BJ Tel: 020 7628 7060
www.icaew.co.uk

Institute of Chartered Accountants in Scotland
CA House, 21 Haymarket Yards, Edinburgh, EH12 5BH Tel: 0131 3470180
www.icas.org.uk

Institute of Directors
116 Pall Mall, London SW1Y 5ED Tel: 020 7930 1949 **www.iod.com**

Institute of Interim Management
'Dolphins', Elmstead Road, West Byfleet, Surrey KT14 6JB Tel: 0870 242 0814
www.ioim.org.uk

Institute of Management Consultants
3rd Floor 17/18 Haywards Place, London EC1R 0EQ Tel: 020 7566 5220
www.imc.co.uk

Institute of Patentees and Inventors
Suite 505A Triumph House, 189 Regent Street, London W1B 4JY
Tel: 020 7434 1818 **www.invent.org.uk**

Institute of Practitioners in Advertising
44 Belgrave Square, London SW1X 8QS Tel: 020 7235 7020 **www.ipa.co.uk**

Institute of Trade Mark Attorneys
4th Floor Canterbury House 2-6 Sydenham Road Croydon CRO 9XE
Tel: 020 8686 2052 **www.itma.org.uk**

The Law Society,
113 Chancery Lane, London WC2A 1PL Tel: 020 7405 9075 **www.lawsoc.org.uk**

London Chamber of Commerce & Industry
33 Queen Street, London EC4R 1AP Tel: 020 7248 4444
www.londonchamber.co.uk

Market Research Society
15 Northburgh Stree,t London EC1V OJR Tel: 020 7490 7911 **www.mrs.org.uk**

Maxwell Batley Solicitors
Fao I W R McIntyre – Head of Corporate Department
27 Chancery Lane, London WC2A 1PA Tel: 020 7440 4400
imcintyre@maxwellbatley.com

National Federation of Enterprise Agencies
Tel: 01234 354055 **www.nfea.com**

Office of Fair Trading
Fleetbank House, 2-6 Salisbury Square, London EC4Y 8JX Tel: 020 7211 8000
www.oft.gov.uk

Office for National Statistics
Cardiff Road, Newport, Gwent NP10 8XG Tel: 0845 601 3034
www.statistics.gov.uk

The Patent Office
Concept House Cardiff Road Newport S Wales NP10 8QQ Tel: 0845 950 0505
www.patent.gov.uk   www.intellectual-property.gov.uk

Scottish Enterprise

South Altantic House 150 Broomielaw Glasgow G2 7JP Tel: 0141 228 2000
www.scottish-enterprise.com

VAT

H M Customs & Excise Tel: 0845 010 9000 **www.hmce.gov.uk** (Now merged with
Customs and Excise to become HM Revenue and Customs Department)

Welsh Development Agency (WDA)

Plas Glyndwr, Kingsway, Cardiff CF10 3AH Tel: 0222 222666 **www.wda.co.uk**

(For working in retail, see the 'Working in Retail' links on
www.bbc.co.uk/education/izone/working/retail/links/html

Plus

- Talk to all the **clearing banks** for advice and business start-up information, together with new bank account details.

- Contact other local sources of advice, including the local government offices, business centres, and Chambers of Commerce, together with any local branches of relevant national organisations. Check out their websites for up-to-date information and/or information packs they can send you.

- Check out Google, Yahoo, Jeeves, or any search engine for the phrases 'entrepreneur' or 'business advice' of 'Business startup' or 'small business assistance' or 'business enterprise' or similar. Look at **www.careersdirect.com** and other career advisory sites.

- Some advice may be free, e.g. from government organisations or from firms promoting their business. Consider attending business seminars and meetings of networking organisations etc.

- Finally, your own accountant, lawyer or other professional may, either through the firm's own client base or its network of contacts may be able to introduce you to potential funders, both private and institutional.

Index

References are to paragraph numbers and to the appendices